# A COACHING JOURNEY

## True life stories of coach training

DIANNE BOWN-WILSON

Published by Phosphorous Press
Lower Farm Barn
Lower St
Islip
Oxfordshire OX5 2SG

www.phosphorouspress.co.uk

First published in Great Britain in 2004

ISBN 0-9549229-0-5

Designed and typeset by Oxford Designers & Illustrators
Cover design by Maria Marsh
Printed by Biddles Ltd

# Contents

# Foreword

THIS BOOK is a bit like climbing Everest. I wrote it because it was there – waiting to be written.

I make no apologies for its rather messy format – this is a book about people and their stories and the way they relate both to an organization and a process. It's about the commonplace and the ordinary and the extraordinary and inspiring all at once. It's about normal, down-to-earth, regular people and I wanted their own voices to be heard – so I structured the book so that they could be.

But people, no matter how *ordinary* they are, are also always absolutely *extraordinary* in some way, more so if they're involved in something as diverse as coaching. So none of it is straightforward but all of it – in my opinion – is quite fascinating.

In fact, this book is three stories in one. It's a story about how a few people with a vision set up a business which became an instant runaway success, proving just how much their approach was right and the time had come. It's also a story about coach training and who does what in order to gain the experience and accreditation that enable them to confidently announce, 'I'm a coach!' Equally it's a story about people's lives – all the people who have contributed to this book who in some way have had their own lives and the lives of those around them transformed through coaching.

My motivation for writing the book came initially from wanting to find answers to a number of questions which had niggled at me since the time I first started to take an interest in coaching:

- Who are these people called 'coaches'?
- What special skills and aptitudes do they have that sets them apart from everyone else?
- What did they do before they became coaches?

- Why were they motivated to follow this path? How do you know if you'll make a good coach?
- How do you train?
- How difficult is it?
- What do you DO when you are a trained coach?
- Is the end result worth the effort?

My own coaching journey started back in 2000 when I came across a copy of Fiona Harrold's book *Be Your Own Life Coach* in the local library. I've always been a devotee of self-help books but this one was different; I tried some of what was in it and … it worked! In fact, it worked so well, that I even bought a copy for a friend of mine who was struggling with some issues. 'Read this,' I said, 'It really makes sense.'

Round about the same time, in developing my own business as a marketing and management consultant, the concept of coaching started to present itself more and more frequently. I started to notice an increasing number of articles and references to coaching in the workplace and saw that increasing numbers of consultants were offering 'coaching'.

My own business model is founded on the premise that any business needs to create and maintain a balance between marketing, management and motivation in order to thrive, grow and prosper. As part of the 'motivation' aspect, I found myself increasingly inter-relating with clients in a way that was, in as much as I knew about it, 'coaching'. However, it made me uncomfortable to say that I was a coach or to offer this as a service without a firm foundation of training to base it on.

In 2002, my then business partner and I were commissioned to write a book on our business model and were forced to do some research on coaching – we knew it was a key part of the management and motivation process and we knew we needed to know more. So we found out enough to complete the book and life moved on, leaving me with a note 'Find out more about training to be a coach' on my sometime/never 'to do' list. I didn't seriously anticipate taking it much further until fate or the Universe (of which you'll read more later) decided to take charge.

Zip forward to Christmas 2002 when my daughter and I went on holiday ('home') to New Zealand to catch up on seeing the family and in my case, recharge my batteries and seriously focus on relaxation and sleep...

I always find this a great time of year for stepping outside the box; the enforced 'time out' provided by the long Christmas and New Year holiday being a good chance to take stock, reinforced by the feeling that one ought to be making some sort of New Year's resolutions. Anyway, to cut a long story short – I flew home from New Zealand in the first week of January having resolved (as I have hundreds of times before) to do things differently and make some changes.

As part of 'catching up' with the world when I got back, I bought the local Oxford newspaper to see what was going on locally and the Universe stepped in by drawing my attention to an advertisement promoting a coaching open day the next Saturday. No cost, no obligation, and no excuse not to go. It was at Eynsham Hall which until then I'd never visited – so with no great feeling other than that it would be a nice chance to see the Hall, find out some more about coaching and do a bit of networking, I decided to go. The rest, as they say, is history.

The afternoon was full of surprises. I was surprised that I was greeted like a long lost friend and made to feel special and valued. I was surprised at the genuine enthusiasm and openness of the coaches there – particularly Natasha Palmer. I was surprised at the incredible good humour and feeling of camaraderie which everyone seemed to be drawn into. I was surprised that I was allocated one person from Rivas Palmer, the company hosting the event, to spend time with me to find out what I wanted to know about coaching. I was surprised how much I liked that person (it was Pam Stokes, now Head of Distance Learning at Rivas Palmer) and how open she was about her own experiences: And most of all, I was surprised that, at the end (or in the coming days) I wasn't sold to. All that effort they'd put in and they just let me walk away to make my own mind up. I was hooked!

Too much research always sends me into a state of dithery uncertainty, so after a few days of thinking about it, measuring the idea against a few internal criteria and checking out my own motivation (certainly determined that I wasn't going to go off down this path and lose interest half way), I decided to go for it. I elected for the March 2003 residential weekend, and having at the outset determined that I would finish the course in the shortest possible time (in order to maintain maximum motivation), I completed the work and gained my accreditation with distinction at the end of July.

My comments on various aspects of the course are interwoven with the other con-tributors' throughout the book, but as an overview I can say here and now that the course was interesting, challenging, well thought-out and well paced, and that the level of support and interest shown in you right throughout the process and even after accreditation, is fantastic. I didn't feel the need to take advantage of very much support, but I certainly felt that it was there if I needed it, and I never felt that those providing it were doing so under sufferance, because they 'had to'.

Since 'graduating' I've stayed touch with Rivas Palmer as most coaches do, and recently have become closer to them as they have undergone some major changes. It was from this involvement, and the opportunity it gave me to take a broader perspective on the whole operation and the people who were involved with it at every level, that the idea of writing this book grew.

Actually, let's just take a step back here. In fact, the idea of publishing the book came out of coaching itself. As I mentioned, the idea for the book was there but there is a vast gap – as any aspiring author knows – between an idea for a book and finding someone prepared to publish it. Particularly something as idiosyncratic as this.

So here I was a few months ago, struggling with how to develop my business and achieve some clarity about what I wanted to do with the rest of my working life. During a one-off coaching session my coach asked me a question which caused one of those light-bulb moments that coaching is renowned for. 'What do you actually want to do?' she said (or something very like it) and just like that, I said it out loud: 'I want to publish books.' Odd that, because until that moment I hadn't really considered publishing books, though I'd thought a lot about writing them.

But, suddenly that was it. And so right! Things moved on from there and this book is the first of what I hope and intend will be many thoroughbreds to emerge from the new publishing stable which is *Phosphorous Press*. Everything is falling nicely into place and all the coaching tenets you will read about, for instance the Universe providing what you need, when you need it, all seems to be coming to pass and helping move the project along.

There was something in Fiona Harrold's *Be Your Own Life Coach* (the coaching book that first hooked me in) which really struck a chord when I read it and summarises what I am trying to base my life around now. She wrote:

*'What makes that vital difference (between good results and stunning results)? Over my years of working with hundreds of clients … I can tell you what it is with absolute certainty. It is the degree of commitment to themselves and their goals that each client has. This commitment is made up of four elements:*

- *motivation*
- *self-belief*
- *self-discipline*
- *willingness to change.'*

Coaching can help you achieve all these things, so if you are currently struggling with problems or uncertainties which are holding you back or dragging you down, I suggest you think seriously about investing in some coaching in order to help you see the way forward. Coaching *is* for everyone, although obviously the subject matter of this book – training to be a coach – isn't. But I've never met anyone yet who in the hands of a qualified and experienced coach didn't achieve significant benefit.

If you're currently trying to decide whether to train to become a coach, I hope the stories in this book and the commentary in between will help you come to a decision. The book is not intended to be a sales pitch for Rivas Palmer, but as you read through I hope it will become clear why it figures so heavily throughout. Undoubtedly there are other organizations which also provide quality coach training, but this was never intended to be an unbiased overview of the entire market – just the story of one organization and the difference it has made to many people's lives.

Finally, as you read through these pages, I hope you will see how coaching has been the common thread which has changed many different individuals in a variety of ways, in some cases completely transforming their lives and those of the people around them. Even if you're only seeking small changes, I believe that if we could all live our lives with more motivation, self belief, self-discipline and a greater willingness to change, the world and everyone in it would be a better place.

*My wholehearted thanks go to everyone who contributed to this book and their support and encouragement for the project. Additional thanks go to Annette Iles for editing beyond the call of duty, Pete Lawrence and the team at Oxford Designers & Illustrators for production, Maria Marsh for cover design and of course, all those at the heart of Rivas Palmer (particularly Natasha and David). I couldn't (and wouldn't) have done it without you!*

Dianne Bown-Wilson
August 2004

# Introduction

Businesses and coaching professionals must join together to push for greater professionalism across the industry. If pressure is exerted to secure minimum expected standards, qualifications and results, the 'cowboy' operators will have no option but to conform.

CHARTERED INSTITUTE OF PERSONNEL AND DEVELOPMENT

NATASHA PALMER is the head of Rivas Palmer. It was her vision and drive which led to its formation in 2002, and she is universally acknowledged to be the organisation's leader, chief coach, motivator, driver, and essential heart and soul. Although only in her thirties, she has created in Rivas Palmer a business which many older more experienced entrepreneurs would envy.

She has succeeded where many others would have failed because of her huge personal charisma, infinite capacity for hard work, and unshakeable belief in the power of coaching and the quality of the services Rivas Palmer offers.

Natasha strives tirelessly and enthusiastically to realise her ambition of making coaching more accessible to all, and manages to do so with an infectious enthusiasm, warmth, and understanding which not only attracts people to her but motivates them to stay and share her commitment.

Throughout its short lifespan, the business has undergone a number of changes, as is to be expected in any organisation which grows rapidly in a market which itself has seen phenomenal expansion. Indeed at the time of writing this book there has been a name change – from the *European Coaching Foundation*, to *Rivas Palmer* as part of a drive to become a completely global organisation. There are also changes afoot to introduce a new modular course programme designed to ensure that the training on offer fully meets changing market needs.

Natasha is generous in her praise for her team, and is the first to admit that she could neither have established the business nor grown it so rapidly without their support. However, they in turn readily admit that it is she who motivates them, inspires them, keeps the show on the road, and ensures that everything is, always, 'alright on the night'.

This, in her words, is the story of how it all came about…

## The beginning...

On the day of the first course when I walked into the room where everybody was seated waiting for me, there was a moment when I just looked at Pam and both of us had tears in our eyes. We both felt, 'My God, it's happened!' After months of hard work and blind faith in the instinct that this was the right thing to do – here it was.

From the easy atmosphere, you would not have believed it was our first course. It was run the same way that the courses run today. But for us, it was new, exciting, thrilling, and a phenomenal success. It was praised across the board and suddenly it took off; it just took on a momentum of its own and soared.

Some months before when we first had the idea to set up, our unique selling point was that we had 18 founder members – trainers and mentors that could definitely do the job; plus a pool of detailed knowledge of what type of training was available internationally. So we felt we could plug all the gaps and were ideally placed to design a better programme and fill what we felt was a huge need for quality training which really equipped people to coach.

What we felt really set us apart initially was the real *passion* for coaching that came through from all of us; the real essence of 'what coaching is about' that we felt wasn't anywhere else. Yes, you could just go along and learn coaching skills from a training organisation, but it didn't mean anything. There wasn't really a family network anywhere and that's what we wanted to create.

We wanted it to be a Foundation, not just a business being run by and for one or two people. We wanted to focus on how we could bring in all our combined knowledge, passion and excitement for a profession that was very new and exciting; contain it, and deliver training in that way. But at the same time we knew we wanted to keep things very real for people, not create something pink and fluffy – so we concentrated on making our business a community and making it the very best it could be.

In hindsight, it was very scary, but at the time that never came into it, because it felt so right. It was almost that this was bigger than us and we were being challenged to put it together. We were in a position that people trusted us and came to us so, for example, we didn't have to advertise for trainers – everything just fell into place. It was as if it was meant to be.

Without us seeming to have to do too much, it gathered momentum and increasingly, every step of the way, we found that it all slotted together. We knew what we were doing and we were doing it for the right reasons, we had the right intentions behind it. We've never wanted to be the largest, but we wanted to be the best. We wanted to give the best quality training, and afterwards to be there still for people as well.

Of course, underpinning the business was the whole ethos behind coaching. Coaching is all about how you can make your own life better and then, when you do, there's a ripple effect. If you're happy everybody else is happy around you; you can help somebody if you're in the place to be able to help them. To me, that's fundamentally what coaching is all about. It's not necessarily training to become a coach, it's training to enhance your life and the lives of those around you.

My journey to starting up the business began a couple of years earlier in 2000. At that time I was working in management in retail but lacked support from my bosses and had just had enough. Very impulsively I handed my notice in and that was it. I had no idea what I was going to do, but fate stepped in with a nine month temporary job to tide me over while I made up my mind.

Six months into that nine months I still didn't know. My mind kept going round in circles thinking, 'Well I could do this, I could do that' – but I never once sat down and thought, 'What do I really *want*?' I was still pursuing the rat race, my ambitions all seemed focused on finance and lifestyle; I never asked the question, 'Out of my whole life so far, what's been the most important thing?'

Then one day my sister said, 'I think you could benefit by being coached.' Me? Coached?

She said that a friend of hers, Sian (Sian McDermott, now a Rivas Palmer trainer and coach mentor) was training to be a life coach and I should have a conversation with her so she could explain it in more detail. We met – and although at that time I was totally green about coaching – she spoke with such enthusiasm and passion that I ended up thinking, 'Hold on, everything she's talking about is what I'm interested in.'

I arranged to have four coaching sessions with her and right from the first session I was bowled over by the whole thing. One of the issues I focused on was that I had done things for other people for 30 years, and I always put everybody else first – and yes, this had made me happy. But then it gets to a certain point where you think, 'Well hold on, who's putting *you* first?' And that's when you realise that actually the only person that can do that is you.

After the session this realisation started to come out in things I decided to do. Some of them were really quite superficial things – for example, I hadn't ever had a smear test, yet I knew it was something I should do for me. So I went along, had it done – and found out I had cervical cancer. I don't want to dwell on it, it happened, I was treated, I got over it – but you can imagine, it was a huge turning point in helping me decide where my life needed to go.

I decided to follow Sian's example and train as a coach.

## The middle...

It took me three months to train, but after that I was just playing shop – the work didn't come in. I felt that when I was coaching I was just helping somebody; I couldn't get it into my head that it was a *business*, that in order to be able to keep going I needed to earn an income from it. There was also the problem of my basic lack of confidence. If I had been working for somebody else I could have sold anything as long as I believed in the product or service. But I didn't believe in myself, I didn't feel as though I was worth £100 an hour and I couldn't ask for the money.

After a while, through various contacts, I became involved in an organisation which held workshops for coaches in building a business as a life coach. It was quite an eye-opener for me and that was when things really began to turn a corner. We used to have people come along who hadn't had a paying client in two years; but after they did the training, things would start to change for them. For example, one of them came along on the Saturday, and on the Monday e-mailed to say she'd got her first client. Amazing!

After this intensive business training some very successful coaches started to appear. It was from here that all the founder members came for Rivas Palmer.

The idea for starting the business emerged from the growing realisation that coaches were saying that the training they had received had given them coaching skills but not marketing and sales skills, no input into personal development and spirituality, and little proactive ongoing support. So to help protect the future of the profession we decided to form Rivas Palmer in order to address these failings and do things better.

Our whole approach to coach training is firmly founded in reality, and we believe our students benefit from this enormously. For example, we stress that coaching is ultimately a step process. Just because you train as a coach doesn't automatically guarantee you a business and a new life at the end of it.

If you come to coach training thinking 'I'm going to be a millionaire, as soon as I have trained', you're coming into coaching for the wrong reasons. Training to be a coach is a personal development journey as well. You need to look at yourself and make certain changes – some of which will be very difficult and challenging. This is fundamental to 'walking the talk' and the attraction principle – both of which I believe are essential prerequisites to becoming a successful coach.

The really successful coaches I know have all taken on board what coaching means and embraced it wholeheartedly, they have all *attracted* their clients to them by living what they believe. It's not something everyone can do, and by racing in and giving up the day job, you're putting so much pressure on yourself by that need to earn money that you probably won't succeed. Your whole focus becomes the money; you're not going through the process of it at all. That's why so many newly qualified coaches find it so hard to get going in business – I really believe that wholeheartedly.

## The future...

Our aim as an organisation is to spread the true meaning of what coaching is and it's through this that we have attracted the people we're working with to us. We live and promote the real essence of coaching and look to create the greatest good for everyone involved.

The marketplace and the world has undoubtedly changed since we first set up, and a lot has changed for us as a business. But that hasn't meant our core values have needed to change. We intend to maintain and develop a platform to spread the message about coaching and in the next couple of years one of our aims is to successfully introduce a coaching culture to commercial organisations that can benefit from it, having concentrated to date on training individuals. Our corporate coaching courses and in-house coaching programmes will allow business leaders to see that coaching really can effectively replace traditional management styles and that the potential for people to perform better is enormous if there is a coaching programme in the workplace.

Currently 'coaching' is a word that's being misused left, right and centre. Management consultants are using I because it's a buzzword, but they're not coaches and they're not coaching. And some people in the workplace are also misusing it. They're advising, they're mentoring, but they are *not* coaching. Just look at any recent research on coaching in the workplace – it says that coaching isn't quite right at the moment. I absolutely agree with that because what a lot of people are doing under the banner of 'coaching' is not right either.

Coaching certainly needs to be regulated before it can be properly and fully adopted as a viable management alternative. Here at Rivas Palmer we're proud of being at the forefront of pioneering higher standards, but obviously we are just one organisation. There needs to be some kind of legislation if we as an industry are seriously going to introduce a coaching standard in the workplace.

Because the word is being misused there's a danger that a lot of damage will be caused, as happened with counselling which is now regulated. I firmly believe however, that even though certain people have jumped on the bandwagon and misused the term to cover what they're doing, true coaching will be around forever because it does enhance people's lives. We know it works. And that's where our unshakeable belief comes from.

People have said coaching is a new religion, but I don't know that I'd agree. Certain religions just expect people to follow their doctrines and not ask questions and coaching's not like that at all. Coaching stimulates thinking, so I guess some sections of society could find that potentially a very big threat. With coaching it doesn't matter what religion you are, as long as you can accept that you do have choices and you're in control. You make decisions because you've thought about things, not because somebody's told you to think that way.

So my message to everyone, no matter who you are or what you do, is that it's important to design the life that *you* want. I wanted to work with friends; I didn't want to work every hour God or the Universe sent me doing something that I wasn't particularly enjoying. I wanted to have fun, to create life/work balance, and to enjoy my working relationships. And that's what I have been able to do through coaching. Setting up Rivas Palmer has really enabled me to focus on enjoying the journey and not being so concerned about the destination.

Our ultimate aim at Rivas Palmer is to infiltrate coaching everywhere, in every organisation and institution, and into people's daily lives. A coaching approach becomes a way of life for those involved with it and I think it's what the world needs. Society today moves so fast that there's no time for anybody, but coaching creates time for the most important person – you.

At the moment Rivas Palmer is still very young. That little seed we started off with is still only so high – but we will become an oak. That's the journey we've got before us. And then – a long time after we, the founder members, have gone – hopefully Rivas Palmer will still be flourishing, because of the foundations that were set at a time we knew was exactly right.

We hope that through this book you will come to understand more about coaching and the effect that it can have on every person's life. Perhaps in time, if you haven't already embarked upon it, you too will undertake a coaching journey of your own.

Natasha Palmer
*Managing Director*
Rivas Palmer

# 1 The meaning of coaching

> You can analyse the past but you have to design the future. **EDWARD DE BONO**

UNTIL RECENTLY, most people had never heard of coaching. Now, TV and radio programmes, newspaper and magazine articles, and even the experiences of friends, neighbours and workmates all ensure that the magic term 'coaching' keeps popping up in the public domain. But what exactly *is* this 'coaching' that we hear so much about? What's behind the process? Why has it suddenly gained such profile?

Ask people what they understand by 'coaching' and you'll get a wide variety of answers including 'It's just having a conversation', 'It's like training', 'It's telling people what to do'. As none of these is accurate, it may be helpful first of all to look at what coaching is – and what it isn't – so that if you're reading this book and are new to coaching, you'll at least have a better idea what the contributors are talking about!

## Coaching defined

There are many definitions of coaching but these seem to me to be particularly useful and enlightening:

'Coaching is unlocking a person's potential to maximize their own performance. It is helping them to learn rather than teaching them.' TIMOTHY GALLWEY

'Coaching focuses on future possibilities, not past mistakes.' JOHN WHITMORE

'Coaches help people become more than they realize they can be.' JAMES A BELASCO

What these definitions demonstrate are some of the key features of the coaching process:
- It's a forward-looking process – unlike counselling which dwells on the past.
- It crosses cultural, gender, age, and socio-economic boundaries and by definition, applies to many different situations.

- It focuses on maximising performance, whatever that performance relates to.
- It works by 'unlocking the person's own potential', rather than providing solutions based on the coach's own experience.
- It is learning-based rather than teaching-based; the coach need have no prior knowledge about the issue on which their client is focusing.
- It enables the person being coached to move forward and change in respect of just about any issue in their life.

## The boundaries of coaching

Another way of understanding what coaching is, is to look at what it is *not*. Coaching evolved from sports training, as is reflected in the dictionary definition of 'coach' – *to train (team or person) for contest.'* However, it is important to realize that coaching isn't *training* in the accepted sense of the word – rather the opposite, focusing as it does on encouraging individuals to learn and to find their own goals and way forward (whilst training is an instructional, teaching process).

Coaching also is not *counselling*, so is not suitable for those with deep-seated emotional issues relating to, for example, physical or mental abuse, drug or alcohol addiction or serious behavioural problems. These cases need help from therapists with specialist skills. Nor is it *mentoring* where the mentor is an expert in their field and provides a role model for someone less experienced; a coach need have no knowledge of their client's field of endeavour. So neither is it *consulting* where someone is retained specifically for their specialist expertise.

## What coaches do

A third way of understanding what coaching is, is to look at what coaches *do*. The role of the coach is to believe in their client and their ability to change, and to be a non-judgmental source of support at all times. The coach will help their client identify which issues in their life (personal or business) are causing them problems and assist them in prioritizing which to tackle first. They encourage clients to set SMART goals (Specific, Measurable, Achievable, Realistic and Time-bound) in order to help drive change; and will help them look at their current situation and what they might need to change in order to achieve their goals. They also help their client identify various options in respect of what they might do and support them in deciding the way forward. Throughout all of this the coach provides empathy, feedback, encouragement and a totally objective viewpoint.

All of this becomes clearer in this account by a leading coach and Rivas Palmer trainer who gives her view of the meaning of coaching and an insight into the impact it has had on her own life:

# What does your life look like?

SARAH STRONG

66 Imagine a picture frame. If it were filled with a picture of you and your life right now, what would it look like? Think what would be happening and what your expression would be.

Now imagine that when you are asleep tonight a miracle occurs and you are transformed into the person you'd really like to be, having your ideal life. You can be, do or have anything you want. Because you were asleep you don't know that the changes have taken place, so how will you know when you wake up? Just what will be different?

For me this exercise sums up what coaching is all about – helping people to work out what they truly want from life and then helping them to make that transition for themselves. It is simple, it is empowering and above all, it is effective.

When we are children we believe that we can be anyone we want to be, anything we can achieve. But as we grow up we develop inhibitions and negative self-beliefs (that little voice inside that tells you that you can't do something) and we start to hold back. Somewhere along the line we lose sight of our dreams and settle for what we have been conditioned to feel is 'our lot'. Coaching helps us to think big again, and to break down those big goals into realistic, manageable and achievable chunks.

The fact is that most of us react to what life throws at us, rather than actively determining the life we want. How many of us end up feeling dissatisfied and believing that we deserved more? Most of our regrets in later life are about what we didn't do rather than what we did. Coaching is about helping people to turn dreams into reality.

Coaches help people to identify what they want, to set powerful goals and then achieve them. I'm sure that at some time in your life you have set yourself a goal or made a resolution and you would be forgiven for thinking 'Why would I need a coach? I can do that for myself!'

However the reality is that many people either break their resolutions and don't achieve their goals, or achieve them and then find they don't bring the level of satisfaction and happiness that they had hoped for. This can be for many different reasons. Perhaps the goal was too big, or perhaps the goal was about what you felt you OUGHT or SHOULD do rather than what you wanted to do.

It could be that achieving the goal hasn't satisfied you because it was not in true alignment with your core values. Are you even sure of what these are? Coaching enables you to work out your values and measure your actions by them.

Sometimes a client will come to coaching because they've reached a crossroads or feel that 'there's more to life than this'. They don't have that bigger picture we mentioned or a particular goal to achieve; they just know that something has to change. Coaching helps people to create that picture and realise what they want from life.

As coaches we give our clients space to really look at any aspect of their life and act as an independent sounding board as they work through their values and goals and brainstorm the options that are open to them. We listen unconditionally – and this is invaluable. You may feel that if you had a problem you would go to friends or family. The trouble is that friends and family think they know what's best for you – what they will give you is well-meaning advice.

Coaching is solution-focused and we are there as catalysts, using effective questioning techniques to help clients come up with their own solutions. Equally, the action that is needed for change has to be carried out by the client, so coaches hold their clients accountable for taking that action. Coaches believe that the only person who knows what is right for you *is* you, but a coach will give you the one-to-one support and confidence you need to take action.

In order to fully understand coaching I believe it's important to know a little about how it developed. It really all started following the publication in 1975 of 'The Inner Game of Tennis' by Timothy Gallwey. The book revealed a different way of helping to improve the performance of sportsmen and women by allowing them to learn through their *own* experiences. Gallwey saw the role of the coach as one who asked questions to help raise awareness and stimulate change.

The idea was developed and explained more fully by Sir John Whitmore in his book 'Coaching for Performance'. Business people who read these books soon saw how coaching could be applied outside sport. And, as you read through this book, you will see how these basic principles of coaching have remained the same.

### Tracing my own journey into coaching

To help you understand the power of coaching, I would like to share with you some of my own journey to where I am today. For many years I worked in the NHS as a therapist. During that time I often saw members of staff treated for stress and I used to think how much better it would be if we could do something to prevent people becoming stressed in the first place.

However, I didn't know what that might be; after all, the stress might be caused by their personal lives and many people like to leave those problems behind when they come to work. Even if the stress was work-related most of us don't want to show our 'weaknesses' to our boss or colleagues. So I concluded that preventing stress and having a genuinely happy and fulfilled staff was nothing more than a pipe dream.

Then my world changed. I got divorced, and with three young children, I suddenly felt the pressure of every day-to-day decision being down to me. I got into a new relationship – I knew it was wrong for me, but somehow I couldn't see a way out. I also decided to move house and bought somewhere that needed major work – it had no functional kitchen, the bathroom was only fit to be inhabited by the many spiders that lived there. With young children that was not a good way to live!

In case that wasn't enough stress, I also changed jobs. Instead of managing a small team of therapists, I took on the role of managing what was then one of the newest hospitals in the country with responsibility for millions of pounds of taxpayers' money – and I didn't think I was very good at it.

I was acutely aware that I wasn't spending enough time with my family, let alone having any 'me' time and that there was no fun in my life. I knew things had to change, but so much seemed to be wrong that I just didn't know where to start. Fortunately, fate intervened. One day when taking my son to the doctor I opened a magazine while we waited and an article on coaching leapt out of the page at me.

That's what I needed! I didn't want someone to tell me what to do, because I had a fair idea of that, but I did need support and someone to listen and help me work out for myself what action to take and when...

Within a few months of being coached I was able to get out of the destructive relationship and it felt like a weight had been lifted off my shoulders. I got agreement to work on a job-share basis which meant I could concentrate on the bits I felt good at and learn from someone else who had the skills I felt I lacked. With my new-found time I was able to do more with my children and prioritise the work in the house – so the ceilings went up, the kitchen went in and we could have a bath – bliss!

### A crisis of confidence

I was so impressed with how coaching had helped to transform me that I became determined to become a coach myself. I didn't do my training with Rivas Palmer (they didn't exist then) – but later they were to transform me from an individual with coaching skills into a successful coach. For me the difference was crucial as the truth is, that after my training was completed I had a crisis of confidence. Well, let's be honest, I had three!

Crisis of Confidence Number 1 – Although I was proud of having gained a distinction in my coach training, I was also very conscious of the fact that no coach had ever heard me coach. A voice in my head kept asking 'How does anyone really know I can coach...how do I know I can coach?' It prevented me from having the confidence to start to market my skills, so eventually, I employed a coach to hear me and give me feedback. I learned a lot this way and I set out to launch my practice with renewed vigour.

Then came Crisis of Confidence Number 2 – I put into place all the marketing skills I had been taught and started to generate some interest in my coaching. People would phone and ask about it and I told them everything; I really believed my enthusiasm would rub off on them. They sounded interested, promised to get back to me, and I never heard from them again – none of them, not a single paying client in three months!

I also found that I simply hated talking about my fees. In the NHS money is a dirty word and I found myself mumbling my costs, almost as an apology. But being the sole source of income for the family I had a real feeling of panic that I wasn't making a go of my chosen career. Plus – I really wanted to make a difference to clients' lives – how could I do that with no clients?

Time for Crisis of Confidence Number 3 – Whilst I was happy to have left the NHS, I found the isolation of working from home very unnerving. I missed being part of a team and was becoming increasingly convinced that, left on my own, I would make no progress and give up.

Then I read an article for a one-day course for coaches that would teach me how to turn potential clients into paying clients. I knew this was a skill I needed if my coaching practice was to survive so I enrolled and found that one of the people running it was Natasha Palmer – a young coach who had already made a name for herself in the coaching world.

The course was a huge learning curve for me. What felt uncomfortable and awkward at the start became a natural process for me by the end of the day. At last I knew the secret of how to build desire for an intangible product like coaching.

As a result of this course my practice blossomed. Now, as well as a healthy client base I also have a regular newspaper column which keeps referrals coming. I specialise in working with individuals post-divorce (that's my passion!) and have contracts to bring post-divorce coaching to the clients of three national businesses. On top of this I also l run a specialist Introduction Agency in the southwest and employ seven other freelance coaches to help individuals find meaningful relationships. Certainly I've come a long way in overcoming those crises of confidence! **"**

As Sarah's story illustrates, coaching is about enabling people to make changes, transform their lives and achieve personal success and fulfillment. As you read through this book you will find many similarly inspiring snapshots of the personal transformations which coaching has helped create.

In telling their stories many people focus on the tangible details of what has changed in their lives – their job, their appearance, the way they conduct their relationships – but as this next story illustrates, what coaching really changes is the way people think. It leads us to question the values underlying the way we do things and creates the motivation for the revolution which then takes place:

> The really great make you feel that you too can become great. **MARK TWAIN**

# Life is like a jungle

MEERA VOHORA

❝ I believe that today, life is like a jungle. We live in a very work-centred culture where we have lost touch with ourselves and have become deeply entangled in things that don't matter. We have huge creative potential that is limited by continual inner chatter and a clutter of information. Because it's easy, we focus on the things that don't make us happy, healthy or wealthy. But with this come anxiety, fear and feelings of helplessness, which lead us to feeling stagnant and stuck.

When I look in front of me, I see this jungle and also I see two very clear paths to find my way out of it – spiritual or material. The jungle represents our life. It has three main layers. The lower part is soil; the middle is plants and the top, the trees. Every element inside it – be it animal or plant – lives and dies because of the other. The jungle is our model as it encourages us to cross from layer to layer and to know other ways of living life.

The question we need to ask is: 'Which path will lead us out of this jungle?' For me, two particular incidents emphasised that life really is like a jungle and that things happen for a reason:

The first was the horrific day of 12 October 2002 when 202 people died in the worst incident ever to occur in the peaceful land of Bali. Both Mike, my partner, and I were there at the Sari Club the night before the blast and only 10 minutes away the night it went off. We both felt that it was necessary we stay on for as long as possible and help in any way we could. It was from then that we knew our lives would change and we had to prioritise our new goals and vision.

It was a journey through hell that over time became a journey of hope and inspiration on a very spiritual island. Somehow, we were meant to be there, somehow we helped and somehow we knew we could never stay on the path we were on – it was time to change direction. It was also important not to let the events embitter our attitude to life.

The second event happened on a routine day when, in the middle of the rush-hour scrum on the tube, I spotted an empty seat with crumpled sheets of newspaper piled on top of it. I pushed my way to the seat and was about to throw the paper away when I noticed an advertisement outlining what life coaching is and what it could do for me. Immediately, I was hooked! I popped it into my bag thinking that this was a perfect role for my partner Mike to pursue, but a year down the line, we both joined the course.

The journey has taken us from being tangled up in the jungle to a path that has led us to change our perception of life through enhancing our performance, productivity and well-being. Building the confidence to find our individuality and to establish where we want our path to lead has been difficult but we're both patient and persistent. It seems that our life map is forever being re-drawn and we are the cartographers.

As the cartographer, you choose the path. Sometimes, like us, you may find a companion on the chosen route that helps support you along the way. Other times, you may decide to take the next crossroads away from those with whom you no longer find any common ground. And at yet other times, you may want to follow completely different directions pioneered by people whom you admire.

For us, it was embarking on the Rivas Palmer course with such a dedicated team of professionals that helped us on this journey of self-discovery. Yes, every now and then we have come across people or incidents that try and put us off-track. But we both know that as we dig inside for the internal changes we want to make, we have the support to get us back onto the path that we have created.

There is a quote from Susan Jeffers that sums up our experiences of life coaching in general, 'The most important thing that you can do for yourself is to follow the path that takes you to the best of who you are. Finding the enormous amount of power and love that lies within is the secret to ending the struggle and dancing with life. So COMMIT to this wonderful journey of self-discovery.' **99**

As you can see, coaching reaches right in to people's souls and for this reason often strays near to what is actually counselling. As mentioned at the beginning of this chapter, there is a very distinct difference between counselling and coaching, although in terms of ethics and philosophies there is much alignment – indeed many counsellors are now reported to be adopting a more 'coaching' approach in their dealings with clients.

The key distinction between the two is that counselling deals with an individual's feelings and deep emotions and stays with the pain; in contrast, coaching focuses on the present and future with an emphasis on performance and visible results. Coaching builds on an individual's strengths and unlocks their awareness and responsibility, facilitating the development of their full potential.

This personal example may help clarify the difference. Many years ago, finding myself in a state of some despair created by the situation I was in at the time, I was referred to a psychologist for some counselling. I went along for several sessions, gave it my best, but then stopped going; I simply wasn't moving forward. Yes, it was initially useful to have someone to unburden myself to, but after that, just focusing on why I was as I was, what had led me to this state and 'how I felt' about things wasn't really helping.

Looking back, I realise that what I needed was *coaching*. I needed to move forward and to see the way ahead and counselling didn't provide that. All it seemed to be indicating was that life was going to be more of the same so I needed to find better ways of coping with it. A valid approach but not very helpful for me when I was looking for strength, inspiration and self-belief.

> Dream as if you'll live forever. Live as if you'll die today.                **JAMES DEAN**

Of course, I am speaking from my own personal experience of some years ago and have no wish to denigrate the very valuable work which counsellors do. However, it seems that counselling often has connotations of either being unwell, damaged, or needing to be fixed. True, many tragedies happen to people and most of us at one time or other will suffer deep grief and anguish over life's events. Surely however, after a period of time, it is better for us to focus on accepting what has happened, looking to the future and trying to move on.

In fact, a lot of the anguish we all experience is to do with the conflict between the 'having' and 'being' aspects of our lives…

## Having and being – which will it be?

**JUSTINE WILKINSON**

66 Erich Fromm is recognised as one of the world's most influential and brilliant thinkers on psychological, philosophical and social issues. In his book 'To have or to be', he argues that in contemporary western society, two ways of existence are struggling for the spirit of mankind.

First – and dominant in modern industrial society, is the 'having' mode, which concentrates on material possessions and power and is based on greed, envy and aggressiveness. The second – and alternative – way is what he calls the 'being' mode, which manifests itself in the pleasure of shared experience and truly productive rather than wasteful activity. It is rooted in love and ascendancy over material existence.

I had not read Fromm at the time I decided to change my own life's course, but I can see that my call to coaching started when I began to recognise that my 'having' mode of existence left me with no time for my life. I realised that I was not 'being' the individual I really wanted to be and that within the life I had built, I was unable to achieve my own full potential.

I do not subscribe to all of Fromm's analysis, however he was one of the emergent philosophers and psychologists prevalent in the 1960s who along with Carl Rogers, promoted theories of personality, development and motivation to a wider audience outside of academia. The coaching process draws on these philosophical principles.

I chose to take control of my life and to be the person I wanted to be by combining my fifteen years management experience with a career aligned to my personal value system, which I came to realise was very much about achieving a work/home balance with time to enjoy being with my husband, children, friends and family. **99**

Now you've read something about what coaching is and what it does, your next question might well be, 'So why now?' What is it about our society at this time, which has created the right breeding ground for coaching?

My belief is that much of the stress and unhappiness which we see about us today simply reflects the fact that human beings aren't designed to change as fast as the inventions we have created. Also our innate competitiveness and drive for mastery and approval means that often we find it difficult to walk away from the rat race and pursue our own – perhaps more altruistic – goals.

Although coaching by no means focuses on encouraging people to 'jump ship' for the sake of it, it is a process which can help every individual question exactly what in our socio-economic system is right or wrong for them and where their ideal life might lie.

## Coaching: The most natural need in the world?

GRAHAM BOOCOCK

**66** Ever wondered why coaching is suddenly such a big thing? After all people have been around for quite some time, so why the explosion in demand for this service?

Starting to understand the answer to this question helped me to appreciate and explain the essence and the universal applicability of the special service that we, as coaches, bring to our clients.

First, a bit of background. I started coaching in the big corporate world, as a consultant and manager in one of the world's largest Information Technology companies. Determined to bring this unique phenomenon to a wider audience by setting up my own practice, I also wanted to develop and hone my skills for the private market. That's when I met the team at Rivas Palmer, from there going on to complete my accreditation and embarking on the challenging business of building my own business.

I knew from my corporate experience the startling results coaching can have, and like everyone else could see the huge growth in interest in personal coaching. Just check out the TV, radio and press coverage, plus the ever-growing 'self help' sections in bookstores.

But one thing kept bothering me – Why?

In any business you need to understand your market and what drives it; coaching is no different. Consultants often say there are five 'why' questions at the root of any problem (see – I knew there was a reason I mentioned my background) so let's give the 'whys' a go:

**WHY No. 1:** *Why is there such a huge growth in demand for personal coaching?*

*BECAUSE people are seeing that it is of great value to them in improving their lives in some way.*

Well that seems pretty straightforward; they wouldn't buy if they didn't see the value they would gain.

**WHY No. 2:** *Why are people suddenly appreciating the value coaching can provide?*

*BECAUSE there may be more and better marketing messages out there – but that's not enough. To drive the messages and the media, there must be some sense that this is about meeting a real need that people know or suspect that they have.*

**WHY No. 3:** *Why have people suddenly decided that they have a need which coaching can address – after all, life is pretty stressful now, but then it always has been.*

*BECAUSE although life has always been pretty stressful, people have previously had different ways of meeting the needs that coaching fulfils.*

**WHY No. 4:** *Why were people able to fulfill their need for coaching before there were professional coaches and why can't they now?*

*BECAUSE the variety of sources of objective, supportive, non-judgmental discussion, which didn't seek to direct but to support and provoke people to find their best ways forward, are ceasing to exist.*

This is certainly a more difficult question than it appears – and takes us to the essence of coaching. What it demonstrates is that 'coaching', in fact, has really been around a long time and is a pretty natural need. Coaching is built on a highly special relationship conducted and managed by someone with time and skills, which are focused exclusively on moving the client forward toward their goals. It is characterised by being:

Non-judgmental

Confidential

Objective

Safe

Free of hidden motives or agendas

Where previously would you have found anything resembling this type of relationship? This required a good deal of thought, but the sudden realisation was 'in many places'. In the traditional extended family where grandparents and older relatives were wise, and had time. Also, in the more nurturing workplace of the past, senior workers would guide the learning of apprentices and support their colleagues. And of course, in older closer communities people had time to care about one another.

Take this further back and suddenly we're at the tribal hearth where tribal elders, wise, experienced and respected, had time to listen and encourage others to explore and focus on a better way.

**WHY No. 5:** *So why is there this huge growth in coaching (isn't that where we started?)*

*BECAUSE our environment has changed:*

- Today's nuclear family has less access to supportive family members
- The workplace is no longer nurturing, but highly competitive and stressful
- Few people live within traditional caring communities

In fact, the supportive 'tribal hearth' has been exchanged for a highly insular, conspicuously competitive and status-ridden modern 'box' where we live under pressure of comparison and fear of failure, with few people truly 'on our side'.

So what do these questions and answers tell us? Well, they told me several things:

- Coaching is a very natural need, which, for eons, has probably been hugely instrumental in helping people reach new dreams and achievements.

- The rise in people seeking coaching is a natural consequence of the way our lives and environments have changed over the last few decades, which has removed many of the traditional types of support.

- Professional coaching has effectively honed an instinctive skill or latent talent, to the level of a professional skill, which allows us to coach people in nearly all situations.

- When people are largely deprived of available coaching-style support, there is likely to be a great rise in the incidence of personal unhappiness, stress-related disorders, frustration and depression (such as has been seen over the last 30 years).

These realisations have helped me to see our profession in a different context, revealing that we are, as coaches, responding to a hugely fundamental human need. **99**

As we have seen above, coaching can create change across groups – businesses, companies, teams – but ultimately it does so through changing each single person. But does this mean that it can be successfully applied to everyone?

Actually no. Although coaching is a valid process for just about every individual in every situation, the crucial point is that it is not an *externally applied* procedure. In order for coaching to be successful an individual must:

1 Take the time to understand what coaching is and what it can and cannot do

2 Really want to be coached and want to change

3 Be prepared to work hard to achieve their goals outside the coaching sessions

That's not something everyone is prepared to take on and it may be that coaching will never be for them. However, for those who can commit, wishes can become reality:

# Turning wishes into reality

ANITA TERBEEK

66 As a human being I had a big wish: to have my own business, which would both enable me to achieve my goal(s) and would respect my core value. That value is *freedom of choice*; the choice to work, walk the dogs or spend time with the family – and be successful in my practice in the meantime. So, what could I do to achieve this?

The answer was hidden in personal experience. Whilst travelling the world for twelve years, I noticed that people from all walks of life approached me. You know those moments; you are waiting for your turn in a shop or a queue and people start talking to you. I never completely understood why this happened but I decided to make a profession of this attraction.

I started training to become an NLP (Neuro-Linguistic Programming) Practitioner and certified in June 2002. But I still felt something was missing. I wanted to do more and was convinced I needed an additional qualification to maximise results. After a long search I found it. I wanted to become a life coach, a profession that was in line with all my personal values and a very good combination with NLP.

It wasn't easy to make a choice between all the different coaching schools, but I felt Rivas Palmer stood out from the crowd. I signed up and went on to qualify as a life coach in December 2002.

It is a decision, which changed my life and one I have never regretted. 99

Each morning when I open my eyes I say to myself: 'I, not events, have the power to make me happy or unhappy today. I can choose which it shall be. Yesterday is dead, tomorrow hasn't arrived yet. I have just one day, today, and i'm going to be happy in it

GROUCHO MARX

# 2 That was then – life before coaching

AS RIVAS PALMER'S statistics show, there is no one sort of person who takes up coach training. Men, women, employed, unemployed, housewives, parents, disabled, married, single … all of life's rich tapestry seem represented. The only thing we disciples all seem to have in common is a tendency to divide our lives into BC (before coaching) and AA (after accreditation)! Of course, for most people there is no neat dividing line; even those who intend setting up in practice as coaches generally find that there is a period of transition.

For us all, learning about coaching and becoming experienced and confident is a gradual process, it doesn't just happen. Even those who felt they had it all figured out before they embarked upon the training admit that they came across a few surprises and many unexpected challenges – and that nothing was ever quite as straightforward as they had imagined it would be.

As you might expect, amongst the trainees there is a good representation of those who have previously worked (or continue to do so) in the caring professions such as nursing or physiotherapy and also those who have been involved in complementary areas such as Aromatherapy or Reiki. Counsellors and trainers are also well represented – either those who are currently employed and want to add coaching skills to their tool kit, or those who want to shift the emphasis of their role towards coaching. There are also a number of personal fitness trainers who want to use coaching to complement their existing skills.

But apart from these categories, the short answer to 'What sort of people train to be coaches?' is 'Everyone and anyone.' Anyone at all, at any age, can train to be a good coach provided they possess the right personal qualities and an unquenchable thirst to learn and develop. Some find coaching is the key to unlocking the door to that magical something they've always known they've wanted to do; others come to coaching through being coached themselves. Some simply find it is the next natural building block for them in a life or career spent helping others.

## A ten-year journey of discovery and development

TIM WATTS

66 By 2004 I had been in the paper industry for 25 years. The business was in the family and I joined after University only stopping at age 39 to ask myself 'Do I want to do this for the rest of my life?'

Certainly I knew that what I didn't want was to look back on my life and career and say 'If only...' So began a ten-year journey of discovery and development that has led me to where I am today.

For the next seven years I worked for The Paper Federation of Great Britain and for the last three as Director of Employment Services. During this time I attended two Anthony Robbins weekends and I also trained with Richard Bandler in NLP. But it was only when I found coaching – joining Rivas Palmer in October 2003 – that I felt I had truly turned the corner.

'People' always drove me and were the most important aspect of everything I did. I used a coaching philosophy at work but was surrounded by many people who didn't appreciate it and who used a traditional 'command and control' approach. However I believe that people respond better to someone taking an interest and helping them to find their hidden resources.

Now my life is accelerating at an incredible rate. I have my own corporate coaching company and life coaching practice. I really feel I can help people create a better life and am certainly doing so for myself.

It's an easy decision to take to move forward – if you have enough reason to do something you will find a way to do it. I may have to change my strategy but I know I will survive because I just feel that where I am now is how things were meant to be. 99

Coach training is demanding and time-consuming. People fit it in around families, travel, careers, other interests and of course, the demands of normal life. For a while during training it seems that everything else is subsumed under the rigours of understanding and implementing the coaching process in the right way, and absorbing and reflecting the information needed to demonstrate that as a student all you have taken in has been 'received, digested and understood'.

However, towards the end of training, aspects of a coach's 'previous life' and/or their existing strengths and interests often rise to the surface to influence the type of coaching they end up pursuing and the niche they decide to develop:

## I had been running fast and furious just to stand still

JUDY McGRIGOR

**❝** My background was initially in teaching and then in writing and producing musical theatre. I lived a really happy fulfilling life with my RAF husband and young children in Cyprus for four years but found it difficult when we returned to the UK to find a career that fitted in with the family. Going back into teaching was a disaster and opportunities in the theatre were not forthcoming.

The eternal maverick, I decided to go into business and thought that Neuro Linguistic Programming (NLP) training would be the best way to get my head together and develop some really useful tools. I loved the NLP training with Paul McKenna and decided that I wanted to combine this with my theatrical and teaching experience to create workshops and courses to help people in their personal development.

What followed was a difficult two years of trying really hard, working on every kind of marketing. It wasn't until my business partner of eight months walked out on me because it was all too frenetic and exhausting (and still no decent income from it all) that I had to stop and do a personal stock-take.

I had been running fast and furious just to stand still – what was it all about? I had a husband and family to consider and myself to look after too.

When I attended the Rivas Palmer open day and met so many lovely 'switched on' kind of people, I simply knew that the training they were offering was first-class. I attended the training course in February 2004 and I received my accreditation in August 2004..

I really enjoy working with my practice clients, they are all getting a fantastic amount of satisfaction out of it and I am so proud of them. I am becoming more and more focused on making positive adjustments in my own life too. I am rapidly discovering that coaching is a vast universe and that there is always going to be so much more to learn.

Through exorcising a few gremlins of my own I am feeling better equipped to 'walk the talk' and by slowing down the pace of life and being more available for my family, there is more harmony and balance, providing a base to work from. I think the very best thing about Rivas Palmer is that I have set the pace and I am supported and encouraged to achieve my targets within my set time frame without any pressures. There is always someone there for me if I need help and they are all people who have been through it themselves so they understand what it is all about.

The marketing workshop was brilliant and I feel confident that when I am accredited and ready, I will be well prepared to win clients, working with people who will really benefit from what I know are my strengths. Looking towards a 'niche', I have decided that I am going to focus on how we can communicate more effectively with ourselves and the people that matter to us.

This could be a person venturing into business or a project on their own, to help them with positive self-talk and communication with clients or associates; anyone trying to combat shyness or having communication difficulties in relationships or at work; or those aspiring to establish really exceptional rapport with any kind of audience. **99**

As mentioned earlier, many people come to coaching having already trained in related disciplines. Although coaching and the models which are held to be at its core can stand alone as a process, coaching can be used very effectively alongside other developmental approaches and techniques, for example, Neuro Linguistic Programming, Learning Styles, Personality Profiling and Emotional Intelligence.

> The future is a concept we invented to avoid facing up to today.      ANON

Although no knowledge of any of these is necessary for someone to become an excellent coach, what tends to happen is that as trainee coaches become more involved in the coaching process their interest intensifies. They increasingly want to know more about what makes people what they are and why they operate as they do.

# I was determined to make changes and do something worthwhile

CATHERINE STRATTA

66 When I decided to train as a life coach, I had been working within the pharmaceutical industry for around 11 years, helping develop new medicines, and was looking for something (I didn't know what) that would be more satisfying and fulfilling.

Having just taken a year out to drive a Land Rover from Cape Town to Tunisia, with many adventures on the way, I had gained some thinking time, and returned determined to make changes, and do something that felt more worthwhile.

I originally took a 10-week introductory course in counselling, but when I saw an advertisement for training in life and corporate coaching I decided to attend a Rivas Palmer open day. Finding it absolutely fascinating, especially the 'hot seat coaching' demonstration (during which a qualified coach took only 20 minutes to help someone sort out an intricate issue) I decided that this was for me. I would have signed up then and there, had it not been for the voice of reason (aka my husband)!

However, on returning home, the more I thought about it, the more determined I was that I could do this kind of work and make a huge difference to people's lives. So after a couple of weeks, I arranged to attend the next available residential course.

Various aspects of my personality have drawn me to this career path. By nature very curious, I have always been interested in what motivates people and the reasons for their actions.

During the early 1990s I was working in project management, and in order to succeed, I had to build and maintain relationships and rapport with others so that they would work with me. To do so, I spent time talking with them (mostly on the phone as I rarely got to meet them) and finding out what motivated them. I took time to learn the best approach for each individual and found I gained a great deal out of these relationships.

Once I had been working with these colleagues for a while, I found that I was able to start predicting behaviours with a reasonable degree of accuracy. I then decided that I could apply this to my clients, which gave me a chance to produce what they were likely to want before they asked me to. This was extremely successful, and I have used this approach for clients ever since.

Since then I have maintained my deep interest in people, and in excellence. I believe that coaching will assist me to broaden these skills and enable me to help others find their optimum path, by raising their self-awareness and supporting them through the changes they choose to make. 99

As you have already seen, many people come to coaching through choice. Unfortunately, however, quite a number are brought to the crossroads through external events such as redundancy, relationship breakdown, bankruptcy, and illness. All can catapult people into a situation where they are forced to stop and think, 'what now'? For many this stage may appear catastrophic, though the majority of people who come to coach training via this route eventually look back and realise that – for them – it was the best thing that could have happened.

## Everything I wanted ... and more!!

DENISE HEATH

66 Having been through two years of disruption in my life – divorce after 19 years of marriage, uncertainty of keeping the family home, returning to full-time work to pay the household bills for myself and my two sons – I was then faced with displacement from Barclays Bank after 26 years of service. Having been involved in staff training, personal development and performance management, I knew I wanted to work in that direction fully, not just playing at it.

I then saw an advert for a Rivas Palmer open day in London inviting people with my personal skills and attributes to attend. I signed up – very sceptical of what would be on offer, but nevertheless feeling compelled to go.

What a transformation I experienced just in that one afternoon! Here were like-minded people who wanted to help other people to achieve their best! They were passionate about coaching, and this shone through in everything they said, and even things that weren't said. Natasha and the others exuded confidence and enthusiasm, leaving me with an energy and excitement I hadn't felt for a long time. I WAS HOOKED!

Yes there was the little problem of how I was going to pay (not having received my redundancy as yet) but I knew I had to be a part of this passionate, exciting company. This was everything I wanted and more!!!!! **99**

As a coach you don't have to have knowledge of the situation or the issues facing your client in order to be able to coach them; in fact your experience shouldn't come into it at all. But sometimes previous experience can not only help us recognise a client's problems more easily, but also help us focus on what is happening or has happened in our own lives:

## My 'issues' were the same ones creating problems for my clients

**ROBIN EVANS** **66** In 2003 I had the opportunity to leave a job that I thoroughly enjoyed but the pressures of which were no longer sustainable. At the time, with a proudly-earned MBA, I was a Purchasing Director responsible for supply chain activity across 12 European sites and a member of the management team running a billion dollar turnover division of a top tier American automotive company. Last year as I completed my coach training with Rivas Palmer, it became increasingly obvious just how out of balance my life at that time had become and equally important, how many of my family and friends my work-focused, cavalier attitude was affecting.

When I started corporate coaching I guess I should not have been surprised to find that the issues that were creating problems for my clients were the same ones that had so absorbed me: the buzz from the job well done, dulled by the feeling of guilt of the real cost, particularly time with my family, for achieving this high level of performance. The elation of the successful negotiation offset later by negative feelings of how much better I could have been. The hours taken to prepare a powerful presentation at the sacrifice of precious time which would have been better invested in my team and their development.

If only I had had a coach to confide in then. Someone who would not only have really listened but also challenged me. Someone who wouldn't have judged me but always supported me. Someone who wouldn't have imposed solutions or given me unwanted advice. Someone whose integrity and confidentiality I could have depended upon; someone who would have helped me develop SMART goals and winning strategies. If only…

All this I am now privileged to be able to offer my clients through my recently launched Corporate and Executive coaching business. To be honest life really is great and a large part of that is due to the support – and patience – of Rivas Palmer. **99**

So the benefits of being a coach are manifest. But before that, the paths that lead people to coach training are as diverse as the individuals who come to it. Some have researched it on the web, some have seen an advertisement, some have read about it, or had their own lives changed by coaching. And sometimes it seems that the Universe intervenes and the idea just seems to arrive. The following stories illustrate just some of the routes by which people arrived at the start of their coaching journey:

## Deciding to become a coach

MARY SEABROOK    **66** One day at work I went to lunch with a colleague, a middle-aged woman who was an administrator in my department. In conversation she told me how she had always wanted to be a teacher, but had never got round to doing anything about it. She was good at her current job, but it wasn't really what she wanted. I suggested to her that life is too short to keep putting off what you really want, and encouraged her to go for it. She talked about some of the practicalities like the money, her family situation and so on, and we discussed what she might do to make it work.

A week later she came into my office and told me she had handed in her notice! She had managed to get into a local college and was going to apply for a training grant. Her husband had agreed to support her, and she was really excited about making the change. She left soon afterwards, took the course and is now a teacher.

I was amazed that one conversation could shift her from always putting off what she wanted to do, to going ahead and making it happen. This wasn't the only occasion either – I had several similar experiences with friends or colleagues, and it made me realise how people sometimes just need a bit of encouragement to give them the confidence to do things that can really improve their lives. Then, when I saw an article on life coaching in a magazine I started thinking that this might be for me.

I thought I would enjoy life coaching because I like hearing people's stories and it is rewarding to feel you have helped people to move their lives on. Although I really enjoyed my job, I had been there for 11 years and at around this time the opportunity to take voluntary redundancy came up. I decided to take it, and have some time off to enjoy myself, do a life-coaching course, and think about what I wanted in future.

I felt that life coaching might suit me because I wanted to work from home, to work part time and to do something that was more worthwhile and fulfilling. I also felt I would have credibility as a coach as I have lived a full life and not been afraid to take a few risks in order to do what I want.

For example, I left my first job as a teacher to travel the world. Some people warned me not to leave a steady job, but I had a fantastic time, and no trouble finding work when I got home. Later I worked for three years in South East Asia, took another six months off to travel, and then changed career. Along the way I tried a whole variety of different things – scuba diving, parascending, learning Malay, Spanish, Arabic, plumbing, lace making, etc. So I felt that I had walked the talk, and could therefore help others – not by telling them about my experiences, but by knowing that making big decisions and broadening your outlook can be easy once you know what you want and start to believe in yourself.

I started looking around for life coaching courses, got information from various training schools and attended a couple of open days. For me, the most important aspects were a course that included coaching practice with direct feedback from practicing coaches; one that covered the practicalities of marketing yourself as a coach (something I had no experience in); and people who seemed enthusiastic about and committed to coaching.

Becoming a coach has helped me in my personal life by giving me more strategies for coping with difficulties; in my professional life by giving me another strand of work; and in my social life by using coaching techniques when appropriate to help my friends and family. Learning to coach is an opportunity to enhance your work skills and your personal life at the same time, and to meet many interesting and dynamic people. **99**

## I knew that it would be a truly valuable journey

ANTONIA BEHAN

**66**Life Coaching was brought to my awareness by a dear friend and fellow life coach, Tonya. When I listened to Tonya sharing her life coaching journey, it sounded so awesome and such a wonderful gift to provide for people, that I knew that life coaching would also be a truly valuable journey for me.

I was looking for some form of professional development, something that would give me the tools, the wisdom and the confidence to motivate and empower others to realize their true potential and live their dreams.

Since my teenage years I have had a passion to uplift others, to provide hope and encouragement and to help people explore their true potential.

My background had been in various industries, including fashion, hospitality and event organising, whilst also offering life path readings in my local town. I was ready to create my own business and wanted a qualification to bring more credibility to my work as a clairvoyant Medium. I also felt that although offering life path readings, where I gave my perception of what was happening in people's lives, was interesting and often rewarding and valuable to my clients, something about it was not quite right, I wanted to give them more.

I knew there had to be another way of working that would empower my clients with the ability to connect with their own wisdom that would guide them to their own personal truth. I am very passionate about inspiring people to discover their inner guidance and to unlock the door to their personal truth in the most empowering way that I can – through coaching. **99**

# The power of positive thinking

HELEN SWANTON

66 Recently I exchanged my full-time job for life coach training with Rivas Palmer. It was a big decision to make and involved me in coming right out of my comfort zone. Here is some of the background to what helped me make that decision.

I was a shy child with little confidence and had been brought up by very cautious parents who often had a very negative view on life. A month before I signed up with Rivas Palmer I was spending a day with my Mum and my thirteen-year-old niece Emma in my old home county of Yorkshire. We went to Harrogate and upon arriving Mum asked Emma what she would like to do. After some hesitation, Emma shyly suggested that she would really like to have her hair cut. Mum's reaction was what I expected; 'Oh I don't think you'll get an appointment today, it's Saturday and you haven't booked' and 'Even if you do get a space, it'll probably be too late in the day.' This negativity went on for some time until I stepped in to rescue the situation.

I am a very positive person now but in Emma I can see the old me. She is very bright but lacks a great deal of confidence. This is something that I try to help her with every time I go back to Yorkshire. On this occasion I suggested quite firmly that Mum go off shopping and I take Emma for a haircut. Mum was a little reluctant but I insisted.

Emma knows my views on positive thinking. Whenever I email her, I send her a positive affirmation to think about. I took her to one side and said: 'OK, Emma, this is an ideal opportunity to see how positive we can be, isn't it? Are you up for it?' (I must admit that Emma is a bit of a 'fan' of mine. She sees me as her trendy Auntie who lives in London and who couldn't possibly be anywhere near the same age as her Mum!) Emma agreed but still quite cautiously.

The first two hairdressers were booked up but we soon came across another. I challenged Emma to walk in and ask for an appointment herself. She just couldn't face it at first but upon persuading her that there was absolutely nothing to be scared of she went in and asked and yes! – they did have an appointment.

Immediately, Emma and the hairdresser struck up a rapport. I hardly recognised her chatting away to a complete stranger. For the first time I was the old Auntie sitting on the sideline watching!

The stylist had not only seen Emma's favourite band in concert just days earlier, but also had some photos with her, one of which she gave to Emma. Then her boyfriend walked in who happened to be a guitarist in a band. This was heaven for Emma who had just started to learn the electric guitar and was mad keen on the idea of playing in a band.

Emma was persuaded by the stylist to go for a complete change in hairstyle and have the trendy cut that she had wanted but had never dared to have. It looked stunning and on top of all this she was given a discount for her next visit.

Emma was on cloud nine when she came out and I took her aside and said, 'So Emma, look at what happened this afternoon. Because we were positive you booked your own appointment, you got on really well with the stylist, you got a photo of your favourite band in concert, you spoke to a real guitarist, you got a discount on your next visit and you have just had the best hair cut you have ever had. *And* you were the prettiest girl in that shop.'

Emma had tears in her eyes when she looked up at me, gave me a huge hug and said (and I remember this!), 'You are going to make the coolest Life Coach ever.'

I think I'm just going to have to live up to that one. **99**

## From reluctant accountant to trainee life coach

KIRK HALINSON

**66** In December 2003, my role was made redundant and I immediately contacted a firm of outplacement consultants in an attempt to define just what I wanted to do in my working career. After an initial discussion with my consultant, I worked over the Christmas period on some questionnaires and the realisation became clear: I no longer wanted to work as an accountant. I wanted do something different – but what?

It was a great boost when, rather than being told to stick to accountancy, I was encouraged to consider a career change. I was given a paper about reinventing yourself and immediately thought 'I can do that'.

Soon after, I saw an advert that read 'A Career in Life/Executive Coaching' and read on: 'Coaching is about moving people forward and helping them realise their potential at work and in their personal lives...' Suddenly I became a 'man on a mission' and started researching life coaching training providers, to decide how best to go about gaining a recognised qualification and to find out more about the whole subject.

Currently, I'm a trainee coach with Rivas Palmer and am embarking on a programme that I know will fundamentally change my working life. **99**

## I found my path in life

KATIE DAY

**66** I was wondering, as you do, what to do with my life, which direction I should go in, should I retrain in something, can I afford it, all the usual stuff, going round and round in circles! Then a friend said to me 'what do you want to get paid for?' A very good question, my answer was 'to help people'. It was easy after that!

I was then offered the chance to be a practice client for a former colleague – funny how life presents you with the opportunities once you've opened your mind to the possibilities. Immediately I saw how beneficial coaching was and knew I had found my path in life. Since that decision and 'light bulb' moment, decisions have been easy to make and to stick to. Now I have completed my training and have loved every minute of it! I can't wait to get going and build, build, build that practice!! **99**

## Now I am truly making a difference

ALISOUN GORT

**66** It was a cold, wet day, the bleak landscape obscured by fog. 'God, I hope this isn't another divorce case,' I thought, already feeling pressured by my tight timetable.

Unfortunately my suspicions were correct; a kindly woman let me into the house and introduced me to a pale and very frail woman whose eyes filled with tears as she looked at me.

'I'm taking her to see a solicitor this afternoon,' the neighbour explained. 'Her 'ex' wants the house sold as quickly as possible.'

Adopting my well-practised Estate Agent professional persona, I assured them that I would measure up quickly. By the time I reached upstairs, I sat on the edge of the bath and cried.

It had been a difficult week full of seemingly endless stories of bereavement, divorce and separation; many hours spent at strange kitchen tables listening to how someone's whole life had suddenly and irrevocably changed. For me it also echoed my own very personal inner turmoil – the absolute agony of loving someone who is unable to love you back. I knew something had to change.

After three years of counselling training I realised in ripe old middle age that it really is okay to express your feelings, not just to put a 'brave face' on life – and that there is no ducking or diving from grief and loss – indeed it is an essential process in our lives. However what happens when the grieving process is completed and you are ready to move on, but just don't know where to start?

Sheer curiosity drove me to attend a coaching open day – I had no pre-conceived ideas. I had come to the end of my counselling course but I knew that I did not want to be a counsellor and was still searching 'to make a difference'.

The pieces started to fit – as Natasha said 'this WILL change your life' and it certainly has. These days I now work as a part-time coach – often helping people move forward after loss – at a level of involvement I was always seeking in my earlier career.

Also, I now work for Rivas Palmer talking to clients and prospective students who often have arrived at the same crossroads that I had. Not only do I really enjoy this work but also the training I have received in coaching has ensured that finally I AM truly making a difference. **99**

## Turning negatives into positives

SHARON DENNIS **66** I have been working in mental health for the last 20 years and have been thinking about a career change for some time. Despite us taking on the title 'mental health' rather than psychiatry in the last few years we often focus on illness and disability and therefore negativity. Working in this area has exposed me to personal development techniques and I am interested in, and told I am good at, mentoring and developing staff.

A random search on the internet led me to discover coaching – which I think is similar to solution-focused therapy in that it is future and goal oriented and therefore has a positive impact on self esteem and so promotes mental health.

I then engaged a coach to help me decide what my next career move should be. Coaching was one of three options and from there I embarked upon the training. **99**

## Utilising potential – mine and others'

GINNY COLWELL

**66** I had been a Director of Nursing for a large acute NHS Trust and from there, moved to become Head of Nursing for an independent healthcare company that included over forty hospitals nationally. Then disaster struck and I was made redundant.

Traumatised, but determined to use the experience positively, I decided not to panic and jump for the next available job but to spend some time deciding what to do. I had become interested in coaching a couple of years earlier but couldn't undertake the training at that time due to work commitments and the fact that I was completing a Masters in Individual and Organisational Learning.

However with the summer free I decided to undertake the coaching course. Until this time I had always thought I had a coaching management style but now I soon realised that whilst I did listen, I quickly went into diagnostic and treatment mode, I never fully utilised the potential of the people I was interacting with; and was much more of a mentor than a coach.

Initially I thought I would incorporate coaching into a new job but when I saw what a difference it could make I decided to include it into a portfolio career. I even coached myself and succeeded in getting the part-time job that I had said I wanted — even before I knew it existed! **99**

> You don't have to be great to get started, but you have to get started to be great. **LES BROWN**

# 3 Feel the fear...

THINKING ABOUT coaching is all well and good. Day-dreaming about being a coach and getting excited about the idea are just fine too. But then… there's putting your money where your mouth is, taking that leap of faith and actually DOING SOMETHING ABOUT IT.

Two of the most common questions asked by prospective students before committing to coach training are:

- Will I be good enough?
- Can I afford it?

These questions in many ways mirror the opposite ends of the spectrum which underpins coaching; at one end the 'people' aspect, at the other, the constraints of reality.

The people aspect is the most interesting if you are fascinated by people. And liking and being fascinated by people is about the only attribute that you *have* to have if you want to be a successful coach. All the rest can be learnt; it really can.

However, at the other end is reality and the practical implications of coach training, which can play a greater or lesser part in people's decision to train as a coach depending on their:

- Financial position at the outset (can they afford the training?)
- Attitude towards the training (do they view it as an investment, or just something they want to do?)
- Overall reason for taking the training (personal or professional development or future career?)
- Support from others (difficult for some people if they don't have backing of employer or partner)
- Overall motivation (do they have the ability to stick at the training, or will they be throwing money away?)

These aren't, by the way, hurdles which the training provider places in prospective students' paths, but they are certainly issues that people are encouraged to fully consider at the outset, to ensure that those who do sign up get the benefit they are looking for from their course, and the satisfaction of achieving their goal.

Probably you are already realising from the personal stories in this book that there is no one type of person who makes a great coach; and no one coaching 'style' that succeeds better than the rest. The most effective and successful coaches all have their own strong personalities, sense of charisma and market niches. Even within the ranks of Rivas Palmer's trainers there are recognizably different styles; some having a more spiritual and intuitive approach, while others are more pragmatic and direct. They are all fantastic coaches and each has devoted and deeply satisfied clients. No one type of coach is better than the rest.

> Whatever you can do or dream you can, begin it! Boldness has genius, magic and power in it. Begin it now.      GOETHE

## The Crufts of coaching

Dog-owner or lover, or not, you'll have heard about *Crufts*, the annual crème de la crème event of the dog world which provides a showcase for an amazing variety of dog sizes, shapes and breeds.

At Crufts you see examples of the incredible bonding and empathy exhibited between (wo)man and beast. Unparalleled? Well, not quite. A dog may be a man's (or woman's) best friend, but after that – surely it's their coach!

Just think about it: Rover is endlessly 'there for you', never downhearted, judgmental or dismissive. He believes in you 100%, listens (never disagrees) and works to your agenda. He challenges, but never criticises, often pushes you beyond your comfort zone (physically or mentally) and motivates you to get up and face the world. Seems the only difference is, he can't ask those really challenging questions…

Taking the analogy a step further – perhaps there is one important lesson to be learned from our four legged friends. That lesson is that a coach's support and devotion can come in a variety of shapes and sizes and still be just right for someone. Whether your coaching style is Great Dane or Chihuahua, boisterous and bouncy, or sleek and subdued – there's plenty of people out there who will be your perfect match.

So, you can aim eventually to be any one of an infinite variety of types of coach, but at this stage of the journey, what are some of the common characteristics students share? Surprisingly, although it may manifest itself in a variety of different ways, or even remain quite hidden, the most common shared trait apart from an interest in people and a desire to 'make a difference' is a lack of confidence and low self-esteem.

## Self-limiting self-esteem

Self-esteem is how much a person likes, accepts and respects themselves; it involves both how we think about ourselves and how that makes us feel. Individuals with very low self-esteem are usually negative in approach, defensive, critical of others, and unwilling to take responsibility for their actions. They also demonstrate a number of self-limiting beliefs, for example, if challenged, they will probably say that they are 'unable to change', 'useless', and 'things that work for other people don't work for me'.

Of course, few–if any–trainee coaches suffer from such low levels of self-esteem, but many at the start of their journey lack confidence and are anxious about whether they're going to be a good coach and whether they'll be able to do what they have to in order to be successful.

Here, one of Rivas Palmer's most experienced trainers gives her view of the importance of confidence:

## On being a novice coach

SIAN MCDERMOTT

❝ One of the best ways of bridging the gap between being a novice and being a confident, successful coach is to walk the talk. Think about who you think a brilliant coach would be, and then aim to be it.

People buy people, not coaching, and they buy people whom they like and respect. So, in order to get people to like and respect us we have to show them something of ourselves and we have to build rapport. All novice coaches should certainly know the theory of how to build rapport from their training and probably will have had some opportunities of putting it into practise – and this is an area which will benefit hugely from sustained practise. Become a master rapport builder. Read books, listen to tapes, try it out when shopping, making phone calls or just travelling on public transport – learn what works and, equally as importantly, what doesn't.

Prospective clients are far more likely to purchase coaching from you if you have clearly got your life together – in other words exhibiting your own belief in the product. No one is suggesting that we have to live a perfect life in order to be a coach, but I strongly believe that we have to be in the process of constantly improving our lives and working on ourselves.

This is certainly something I experienced in my own life (and continue to do so). I graduated as a coach back in the last millennium! Back then coach training courses were pretty basic and certainly offered no help with marketing or sales – we were blithely led to believe that all we had to do to build a sound business was to hand out some business cards, chat to our friends about coaching, call a few businesses, and potential clients would be beating a path to our door to join the waiting hordes.

Having been self-employed for the majority of my working life I was not quite that naïve; nevertheless this was a brand new area for me and I was going to have to sell myself for the very first time. What's more, I had not realised quite how little the world knew about coaching. I really should have done, because six months earlier when I stumbled across Laura Berman Fortgang's first book I had never even heard of it myself.

So there I was, newly qualified, plenty of practice clients under my belt giving me the confidence that coaching worked, but no actual paying clients. Not even the ones that pay you £1 a session so that you can fool your gremlin into believing you really are practising now!

It would have been quite easy to have become totally overwhelmed with the enormity of the task before me and just quietly given up like so many other newly-qualified coaches before and since. Fortunately, wherever I turned the concept of networking filtered into my consciousness. So, like any sensible person who is hit frequently enough on the head with a baseball bat while the coach yells 'Can you hear me yet?', I realised the Universe was trying to get a message through to me. I did a little bit of research and discovered there were numerous networking organisations in my area keen to accept new members.

The first one I visited was the local chapter of Business Networking International (BNI). I had no idea what to expect, but I hauled myself out of bed at 5.30a.m. (I'd forgotten such a time existed), dressed myself in my snazziest business clothes, grabbed my sparkling new business cards and headed off for the venue. Staggering, isn't it, how little traffic there is at that time of the morning?

What a surprise – here was a bunch of local business people, full of bonhomie and startlingly awake for such an early hour, welcoming me as though I were a special guest. They were very keen to introduce me around the group and find out what I did. Despite my lack of coaching experience I was so full of enthusiasm for my subject that those I spoke to were intrigued. I almost forgot that I was a novice coach without a paying client!

I decided to join the network and started promoting the benefits of coaching through the one-minute talking slot that each member has each week and by offering free sessions to all BNI members. I got my first paying client within three weeks and soon was converting BNI members into long-term clients. I don't suppose my new clients had any idea they were to be my first paying clients; it is, after all, a mental rather than physical hurdle that any newly qualified professional has to get over. It does neither our own, nor our client's, self-image any good to labour the point. I am not sure how confident I would feel if I visited a doctor only to have him tell me I was his very first patient – some things are better left unsaid!

There is nothing like momentum to build a business. Soon, I suppose because of my enthusiasm, I was being invited to other BNI chapters to talk about my experiences of building my business with networking – this grew my circle of contacts and of course my clients. The biggest lesson for me was that just joining one of these networking clubs is unlikely, in itself, to get you clients. One has to work hard to make an impression for, make no mistake, it is the coach and not coaching per se that they will be buying.

Just as the old joke goes 'I joined a gym to lose weight, now they tell me I have to attend' you have to do more than just attend a networking event to get a client, you have to work out a bit too. It is a great vehicle for you to raise your profile, and the profile of coaching and to get the members warmed to your product. If there is one major thing I learnt early on it is that lesson that people buy people, much more than they buy coaching.

I took every opportunity to visit other BNI chapters in other towns and my name soon became familiar at those events. I always tried to educate my audiences, whether through one-minute or 10-minute talks, or one-to-one conversations. And by varying my subject matter I was increasing my chances of hitting a nerve with different people –

one might be left cold by work/life balance, but attracted by the prospect of having more self-esteem.

### The power of personal impact

In my years with BNI as Chapter Director and now as an Ambassador, I have come across many other coaches – some doing well, but some plainly failing to win business. So what differentiates one from the other? I believe it is very simple. Consider this, if you wanted to hire a coach, which of the following would you choose?

a. An enthusiastic, active advocate of their own profession, passionate about what they do, trying to live life to the full, who makes a lasting impact on you in the first 30 seconds. A person who looks well put together and who inspires you with their self-confidence,

or

b. A nice, kind person, but one who is slightly self-conscious and who, when asked what they do, utters their pre-prepared elevator speech by rote. There is nothing wrong with their attire, but you are hard pushed to remember what they were wearing and, to put it bluntly, they came across as just forgettable!

Obvious isn't it – well, maybe not to some of the coaches out there trying to get clients. When I hire a coach, I am looking for someone who I can use as a role model in some way and this, I believe, is what others are looking for too.

It has been said to me on many occasions (so I have to believe it is true), that it is my energy, confidence and friendly style of presentation that starts people thinking they might try some coaching. How I present myself, physically and verbally, is important in bringing in clients.

People are naturally slightly apprehensive about hiring a coach for the first time as they do not know what to expect – if the coach comes across as nervous and unsure of themselves as well, it stands to reason they are unlikely to be hired. Who needs two of you stumbling around in the dark?

It is our job as coaches, if we wish to sell ourselves, to raise our level of self-awareness of how we come across to others. I am not suggesting that we all look like Kate Moss, but however curvy or cuddly we might be we need to come across as vibrant and fit. As coaches we need to be in control of our health. I will never forget the one and only time I went to a homeopath – she snuffled and coughed through my whole session – I've never quite got the hang of homeopathy as a result.

If we are not as confident as we might be about speaking in front of a group of people then organisations such as Toastmasters are invaluable – to have the confidence to stand up and speak at the drop of a hat is a great skill.

### You are what you wear

Those new to coaching also need to think about how they look – coaching is a new and dynamic profession and I think that gives us licence to be slightly different from the suited hordes. Shrinking violets are unlikely to make successful one-to-one coaches, not because they are not excellent at their craft, but because in order to sell themselves, they need to get noticed.

Now for those of you who are thinking 'I don't want to make a spectacle of myself' – relax – that is not what I mean. Some of the best money I ever spent was on having my colour and image done by a qualified consultant. Now I know what suits my colouring and personality and I can make the most of both instead of covering them up in some nondescript navy suit.

So having sorted out the rapport, appearance and communication skills the next important thing is to decide how and where you are going to sell yourself. CJ Hayden wrote a brilliant book called 'Get clients now' and I can't think of a better starting point than that to decide what method to use to fill the pipeline with clients.

For those of us who love to talk, networking and public speaking are brilliant; the writers amongst us may prefer to write articles and newsletters and so forth. Just as we need to find the clothes to bring out our personality so we need to choose a marketing method that suits our style. 99

From this, it's clear that training to be a coach doesn't involve losing your individuality and personality, but rather focusing on being the best you can be and dropping all those self-doubts and confidence problems that can stop you being and doing the very best you can. A benefit of this is that the more comfortable people feel in their own skin, the happier they are to welcome others and to share…

## A vibrant and uplifting welcome

ANTONIA BEHAN

**66** When I walked into the training room on the first day of the weekend course, I was welcomed with a vibrant and uplifting energy – a truly positive feeling that these coaches were really passionate about their work. I had a strong sense of being in the right place and could see that they were full of spirit and love, revealing to me the positive and vibrant energy that I had been looking to bring to my own work. **99**

Rivas Palmer's open days have been the catalyst for many students to overcome their fears and self-doubts and convert their interest in the *idea* of coaching into a passionate commitment to becoming a coach.

## Neither cold nor flu could prevent me…

LYNNE SCURLOCK

**66** After reading various articles on life coaching and attending a talk at work, I became very interested and felt that this was the way I wanted to go. When I saw an advertisement in my local paper for an open day in Brighton. I was straight onto the phone to book my place.

When that cold and wet Saturday in February arrived, I could barely get out of bed; feeling terrible, I struggled along for the afternoon session, sending my daughter off with my partner, not feeling in the least bit enthusiastic. Fear of a new situation, compounded by flu – I can only imagine what people's impressions were of me!

Everyone was so friendly and enthusiastic about life coaching. The open day was informative and very well-presented and it gave me an opportunity to ask questions to allay any fears I did have. Although unfortunately I had to miss the final part of the presentation, nevertheless I was hooked! A few days later, having been bedridden with flu, I was on the phone again, booking my place on April's course. It has been a roller coaster of a ride from start to finish, but I am now accredited and feel truly part of the Rivas Palmer family. **99**

One of the most common themes that emerges as students talk about what motivated them to sign up for coach training is the warmth of the welcome they received when they first came into contact with Rivas Palmer and how the simple act

> One doesn't discover new lands without consenting to lose sight of the shore for a very long time.    ANDRE GIDE

of being made to feel 'part of the family' right from the start, overcame their nervousness and misgivings.

## I was impressed by their honesty, integrity and passion

**MARIE STEVENS**

❝ I became interested in life coaching after reading an article in a national newspaper. I started collecting information on different courses but didn't 'click' with any. The right time for me presented itself when I attended an open day in August 2003. I was impressed by the people I met, their honesty, integrity and passion.

These things, coupled with the lack of sales pressure, was what finally drew me to them to for coach training.

My training began in February 2004 when I attended the residential weekend. I met some wonderful people, had a great deal of fun and experienced my first taste of what coaching is all about. Since then I have progressed on a journey of self development and fulfillment as I work towards accreditation.

Working with my clients, listening to what they want to achieve and helping them get there is a wonderful experience. ❞

Some students fears are about the training itself, others' fears are wider. We're all familiar with the saying, 'there's nothing to fear but fear itself', and for one student, this has a particular resonance:

## FEAR... feel it, smell it, taste it, do it!

**LATEEF BADAT**

❝ Although I started my coach training course in May 2004 the origins of my journey began long ago in my quest to address my personal fear of dealing with confrontation – both verbal and physical – and the adrenaline rush that I mistook for fear.

Dealing with any type of fear can be distressing and in my case it was often terrifying and sometimes deeply depressing. My quest to overcome it has led to me studying a number of martial arts, and to hypnotherapy. However I soon realised that there was no miracle cure – which created other feelings of despair and anxiety.

Then, approximately two years ago, two life-changing developments occurred. The first was that I was told about life coaching. I found it interesting and booked my first introductory session. Simultaneously I had come across a person called Geoff Thompson who after spending nine years working as a doorman wrote about his experiences in his book, 'Watch My Back'.

Like myself, Geoff had been looking to conquer his fears of violent confrontation and chose to work as a doorman to help him do so. Using his many years of experience of martial arts and encountering violence as a doorman, Geoff had brought the 'Fence' to the fore, a system of effectively dealing with confrontation.

My first coaching session was very powerful. I got a lot out of it and all the way through I felt that it was going to be the start of something very special. Looking back, it has been exactly that. The coaching relationship was very strong and I knew that my coach was truly committed to my goal. From then on I began developing an indestructible self-belief in achieving it.

My journey then led me to Coventry where I had the opportunity to personally train with Justin Gray (former British & European Vale Judo Champion, full contact fighting), who was one of Geoff Thompson's senior instructors at the time, as Geoff himself no longer taught. The four day training was long and very challenging with ample bruises to show for it, but worth every minute.

I feel that my self confidence and motivation to 'dig-deep' during those rigorous sessions was a result of the coaching I was having. I had progressed a long way in dealing with fear and positively responding to being out of my comfort zone. The highlight was actually meeting Geoff at a Thursday morning, invitation only, session. This experience itself was very motivational, inspiring and emotional. I felt that I was in the right place and had found what I was looking for. The energy in the room was electrifying. It was a further honour when Geoff invited me to attend the sessions on a regular basis and gave me free copies of some of his books.

Since returning from Coventry this experience, combined with the coaching, has transformed the way I live my life. I have experienced changes in my diet, environment, friends, language, reading, and even what I watch on TV!

As my coaching sessions progressed and I spoke about how I now dealt with certain situations and people, my coach asked my permission to make a suggestion The suggestion was that I would make a brilliant coach and that I should look into taking a coaching course.

As a result, after much research into the various coaching training providers, I attended a Rivas Palmer open day in January 2004 and decided to commit to the course.

Using coaching as a tool to help me deal with my fears and progress as an individual has been a life-changing experience. Some examples include getting married in August 2003, and having the courage to resign from a well-paid job to concentrate on becoming a coach.

Even more significantly I have overcome my terror of rollercoasters and thrill rides. From as far back as I can recall my fear of them has led me to feel not only embarrassed but cowardly. Therefore, during April and May 2004 my wife and I (well I needed some support!) took two rides each week at Blackpool Pleasure Beach. I still felt the fear – but it was definitely different.

The difference was that through coaching, I had come prepared. I had thought about what going on the ride would do for me, and how it would make me feel and how it would affect other parts of my life. I used NLP techniques to visualise being on the ride, created my perfect moment and then made it even better, again and again.

To date I have sat on every thrill ride at Blackpool, the best so far being the Pepsi Max Big One, a 74 mile per hour coaster, generating 3.5 G-Force, descending from a 213 foot high crest. To really challenge myself I always ensure that I sit in the front carriage – smile please! Also while on holiday in Dubai during June 2004 I went on the *Jumeirah Sceirah* the tallest and fastest free-fall speed slide outside North America.

Overall I have enjoyed every minute of it and want more! (The thing I am really looking forward to is a tandem parachute jump for Summer

2005) Looking to the future I intend using my experience to work as a coach in a niche area of helping people deal with fears and confrontation, and stepping out of their 'comfort zones' – either in a personal or work setting. Additionally I will focus on helping people to build greater self-confidence, assertiveness and self-belief.

My message will be simple but powerful:

EVERYONE HAS THE POWER TO ACHIEVE THEIR DREAMS…LIVE YOURS TODAY! 99

Finally, prior to starting the course, students are sent a tape or CD on self-awareness to help them deepen their understanding of coaching and put them in the right frame of mind to embark upon their journey. The tape starts, reassuringly, with the statement, 'You don't have to be a perfect person to be a coach', I wonder how often any of us ever go back to that tape or CD to remind ourselves of that?

The minute you begin to do what you want to do, it's a different kind of life.

BUCKMINSTER FULLER

## Think of yourself...

VANESSA WESTWELL

Think of yourself

A day
From now.

A week
From now.

A month
From now.

A half year
From now.

A year
From now.

Think of how
Things will have changed.

The boundless possibilities.
The creation of new life.

The complete release
From old patterns of being
Old ways of seeing.

Think of yourself
And be inspired.

Think of yourself
And rest in love.

Think of yourself
And fulfil your heart's desire.

Think
Be
Do

See.

Become yourself
Whole and free.

# 4 Understanding the theory

> It's a funny thing; the more I practice the luckier I get. **ARNOLD PALMER**

THERE'S QUITE a lot of scepticism about coaching for the simple reason that if you don't know anything about it, it does sound as though it is just having a conversation with someone. How difficult is that?

In practice however, as all trainee coaches will agree, it's far from that simple. At the time of writing this I've just been teaching my daughter to drive, and there are some interesting parallels. I just have to mention to anyone that I'm giving a teenager driving lessons and they roll their eyes heavenwards and say 'Are you mad?' or 'Poor you!' That's because they know, often from painful experience, just how difficult, frustrating and emotionally fraught learning to drive a car can be.

Yet logically, it shouldn't be; after all, none of it is intrinsically difficult. Steering, changing gears, looking in the mirror, stopping and starting, are all pretty easy and straightforward things to do in themselves. It's when you have to do them *all together* in response to whatever road conditions dictate, that it gets hard.

Similarly with coaching. Asking open questions, listening, establishing outcomes and goals, not giving suggestions, keeping to a fixed time slot – these aren't exactly difficult things to do in themselves. It's when you have to do them all in a way that will move the client on and help them achieve insight, inspiration and commitment to a beneficial outcome – all within a relatively short period of time – that you start to feel the heat is on... Not quite 'just having a conversation'.

## Rivas Palmer training programme

When it first set up in 2002, Rivas Palmer designed and ran one comprehensive training programme (it has now gone on to develop a portfolio of different modules). This was suitable both for those who wanted to develop a business in coaching and those who either wanted to take coaching skills back to the workplace or simply use them as part of their own personal development.

Obviously this is only one training course from one training organisation, but I provide the details in order to demonstrate the sort of elements that any good coach training programme might be expected to cover. This one comprised:

- An intensive introductory residential weekend covering all the basic elements of life coaching
- A one day workshop on Marketing and generating paying clients
- Three written exercises
- A number of documented hours of practical work, with a final practical assessment
- On-going email and telephone support from a mentor coach, tutors and support staff throughout the training process
- Information updates about life coaching through the Rivas Palmer newsletter and emails
- Mandatory teleclasses on a range of coaching subjects
- The opportunity to meet and share experiences with other coaches at local/regional coaching Forums

For many, the most life changing of these was the two-day residential training weekend.

This was by no means a traditional, classroom-style training session, but an exciting, interactive learning experience with coaching demonstrations and supervised exercises enabling students to practise newly acquired skills with the support of qualified facilitators.

Before this, the truly keen (or overly anxious) already would have started reading some of the recommended texts in the hope of getting off the starting blocks fast. Nice try, but there was nothing that could really prepare you for the absolute maelstrom of emotion and whirlwind of new experiences that comprised that first intensive weekend...

## Warming up to coaches' glow

ALAN MATTHEWS     **❝** With some people after a while, you can't remember what life was like before you met them. They seem always to have been there. The people at Rivas Palmer are like that. And yet it's not so long since that cold February morning when I wandered into that hotel in Stratford – and started to turn into a coach.

I'd been running training courses for years before I went to the residential weekend, so going into a hotel and finding a seminar room was no new experience. On this occasion, though, I was anxious.

For one thing, I'm a terrible back seat trainer. I'm awful on courses. Really, I'd much rather be up there running the show than sitting listening and participating and I can get quite impatient with presenters (yes, I know that doesn't make me sound very nice, but I'm trying to be honest here). So I wasn't particularly looking forward to being there for two days.

Secondly, I was still wondering 'What are these people like? What sort of people are coaches? Will I fit in?'

Well, when I turned a corner in the corridor and walked towards the registration table, I had my first experience of what I now call 'coaches' glow'. Not the perspiration kind caused by too many people in the same room, more like the old advertisement for Ready Brek where the children go off to school with a warm glow around them protected against the Winter cold.

Coaches have this. Well, the ones I've met do anyway.

They have an aura that comes, I think, from being completely at ease with who they are. I've never met a group of people who are so committed to what they do, so enthusiastic. They're just so pleased to be coaches. For many, it's just what they've been waiting to do all their lives, they just hadn't realised it before. And when they gather together, you can practically see it in the air around them. It's like a group magnetic field, which draws you in. Once there, you can never quite escape.

So, having been greeted like a long lost friend and shown into the training room, I was starting to feel a bit less nervous. These people seemed to be quite normal (well, apart from the glow...). And the others on the course (about 25 of them) seemed to represent a pretty fair cross section of human life. A whole range of ages and backgrounds. So far, so good.

My first concern was then dealt with quite quickly. The trainers on the course were excellent – lively, humorous, knowledgeable. Try as I might, I couldn't really fault them. And they were especially good at handling difficult participants who asked awkward questions and started some light-hearted heckling (well, I told you I was awful on courses).

I'd read a huge amount about coaching and I thought I knew quite a lot about it, after all I'd been a trainer for 13 years or so and I ran sessions on skills such as questioning and listening. But I was mistaken. This course showed me how much more there was to learn about the art of coaching. With a mixture of interactive presentations and practice sessions in threes, we went through the whole spectrum of areas you need to understand to be an effective coach – questioning, listening, building rapport, goal setting, using the TGROW model. We also covered spiritual coaching and self-esteem.

Another question I had in my mind when I went in was 'What's it like to be a coach? How does it feel to coach someone?'

The demonstration sessions helped with this. We watched some experienced coaches running short sessions with volunteers so we could get a sense of what it was like.

The demonstrations were helpful, but our own practical sessions were invaluable. You can sit and listen to someone talking about coaching. You can read all the books you can buy (and there are a lot – I've bought most of them). To know about coaching, you have to actually do it. And to be coached yourself.

That's when you learn what it's like. You learn how it feels to take someone through the process of self-awareness and realisation that coaching represents. You feel the power of coaching. Like being at the wheel of a really powerful car, it's exciting but a bit scary at the same time.

That's also when you learn how much practice you need. The coaches made it look so easy but you soon find out there's a lot more to it. The great thing, though, is that the course makes you so enthusiastic, so keen to learn, that you can't wait to go on and do more.

So this was it, now we had all started out on the road to becoming coaches. What next?

### Putting the theory into practice

One thing we had to do was keep in touch with our 'study buddies'. We had all paired up with someone else on the course and arranged to stay in contact to compare notes, to support each other and maybe even coach each other. In the months to come, this relationship proved to be very important in keeping many of us on track when our initial enthusiasm started to wane.

It's one of the best features of Rivas Palmer that there is always support there when you need it. The 'study buddy' system is an example of this. Also, the fact that you're given a mentor coach to work with during your study. This person will coach you and you will coach them. But you can also call them and ask for advice and help.

This is really important once you get back from the residential course. You then have to find some practice clients, embark on the practical side of the course, and do all the written work. This can seem quite daunting, especially if you haven't studied for some time or if you have family responsibilities (and a job!) to work around.

At one point, a few months in, I remember several of us student coaches attending one of the Coaching Circle meetings that Rivas Palmer regularly organise in Stratford. We were all in the same boat, part way through the course, most of the practical work done but nearly all the written work still to complete. We were a bit tired, a bit overawed at the thought of all we had left to do.

We agreed to support each other through the remainder of the course. We each set deadlines for completing the rest of the work and agreed to email each other to check on progress and give each other a kick if we needed it. That seemed to do the trick. It certainly got me through a sticky patch and spurred me on to finish – which I did five months after the residential course.

I've probably made it sound as if the written work is a great burden. Actually, it's not, it's just that you tend to focus more on the practical side because that's what you want to master. Then you realise there's still the other work left to do.

But it's useful in many ways. Writing about coaching helps when you're putting together marketing materials later, it helps you to organise your thoughts and to answer those challenging questions people ask you like, 'So what *is* coaching exactly?'

### Working with guinea pigs

In some ways the scariest part of the course is when you start to work with your practice clients. These are people who haven't paid to be coached but are 'willing volunteers'. That's another term for 'guinea pigs' although I've found it's best if you don't tell them beforehand that you're experimenting on them.

The amazing thing is, even at that stage, you realise the difference you can make to people. One of the very first people I coached as a practice client gave me the best testimonial I've had so far and still tells me how the sessions helped to change her life. I did a mixture of face-to-face and telephone coaching with my practice clients. Like many people on the course, I was a bit sceptical when coaches said they worked mainly on the phone. I know many of us thought it sounded strange, but the elders of the tribe looked at us with kindly forbearance, smiled knowingly and said, 'Just give it a try.'

And there are certainly things to be said for telephone coaching, especially when you start out. For one thing, no-one can see the mess your desk is in as you spread notes around to remind yourself what you're supposed to be doing.

And they can't see the panic on your face when they describe their problems to you and you're trying to listen, make notes and think of the ultimate coaching question before they've finished speaking. (Of course, after a while, you realise that there is no ultimate coaching question and your best bet is just to listen carefully and trust that the questions will arise naturally. You learn to relax and have faith in the coaching model. But at the start you can't quite bring yourself to do this.)

Another benefit of telephone coaching is that you don't have to rush round making sure the place is tidy and you've cleaned the bathroom before a client arrives. You don't even have to shave, wash or get dressed if you don't want to (OK, that may be more information than you need, I think I'll move on).

### A coach is a wonderful thing to be

After all this, once you get through the course, you find somehow you've managed to develop a certain level of confidence about coaching. The fact that your mentor coach supervises you and that the course is so thorough, gives you reason to believe you can really do this; you are now a real coach.

Actually, it's a bit like a driving test. It's only after you've passed that you start to learn how to drive in a real, practical sense. The course gets you to a point where you shouldn't do any harm and you can be allowed out in public. In fact, you never stop learning about coaching, you never stop developing and building up your bank of experience.

Well, now I continue to run my training and coaching business. I find coaching is gaining a higher profile, although not everyone is clear about what it is. The term 'life coaching' especially, still raises a few eyebrows. People think it might be something to do with swimming. Or you're one of those people they see on the TV who go into other people's houses and say 'Change that wallpaper, don't eat junk food, never wear white socks – and stop letting strange people into your house.'

Still, more and more people are finding out just what coaching is and what it can do for them. And to be a coach is extremely rewarding. If you want to help people, to watch them develop and grow in confidence, to see them take back control of their lives, then 'a coach' is a wonderful thing to be.

Just watch out for the 'glow'... **99**

A big focus for the weekend's training is an introduction to the TGROW model, a simple straightforward process that can be used effectively in any coaching situation, personal or corporate. Nearly all the training provided by Rivas Palmer and many other organisations has this model at its heart.

TGROW stands for
**T**opic
**G**oal
**R**eality
**O**ptions
**W**ay forward

The TGROW model is used to help an individual focus on a specific **Topic** (an issue in their life) and from there, develop one or more SMART **Goals** based around what they would like to change. However, in order to do this, it will be necessary for them to carefully examine their current **Reality** in terms of their strengths, weaknesses, opportunities and threats – and the **Options** that they have in terms of how they might take things forward. From this they can be asked to identify the **Way Forward** in terms of what they will actually commit to doing to help them develop and move on.

> In theory there is no difference between theory and practice, but in practice there is.
>
> JAN VAN DER SNEPSCHEUT

By guiding and supporting their client through this process, an experienced coach can help them:

- clarify the nature of their issue or problem
- examine their current situation in respect of that issue or problem
- discover and evaluate options for moving forward or finding a solution
- set a specific, measurable, achievable, realistic and time-bound goal in respect of the option/s they choose
- commit to a way forward in order to achieve that goal

Sounds simple? It is, but as every trainee coach will agree, it's much, much harder in practice than it sounds on paper! For a start there's a lot to understand about how humans change and learn…

## The nature of success

STEVE ELSHAW      66 Success has been defined as 'the progressive realisation of a worthy ideal'. I concur with this mainly because it implies that success is ongoing. We should constantly strive to set new goals, new targets, new horizons. It is important that we constantly move forward because if we don't, by definition we will move backwards. There is no such thing as inertia.

My life started to change when I began to understand the relationship between the conscious and the sub-conscious mind. As individuals we function on three planes: we are *Spiritual*, we have *Intellect* and we have a *Physical* body. There is a tendency to think that the physical side of our presence is the most important when, in fact, it is the smallest part of us. Our physical actions are only a manifestation of what has been placed in our subconscious mind.

The sub-conscious mind is the most important part of our being. It is our Powerhouse, a tremendously powerful computer. We are what is in our sub-conscious mind. Like any other computer however, it needs to be programmed and herein lies the secret to success.

Our computers have already been programmed; it's called conditioning. Conditioning may be positive or negative and probably began when we were very young.

As we sit back and examine where we are in life today, we should realise that we are a product of our conditioning. The chances are that if you have been brought up in a very positive environment, been the recipient of praise and reward, you will be pleased with where you are today. But if you're not and you need to make changes, you *can* change your computer's programme.

I refer to the 'computer' as a filing cabinet, full of files. If we are to make changes, the files need to be changed. Unless they are, when any thought or idea enters the filing cabinet it will instantly be rejected and this is precisely what happens when people are subjected to *external* motivation such as that experienced at sales conventions and the like.

People leave high-powered conventions believing that they can change the world and themselves only to realize a few days later that nothing has changed. Why? Because the 'files' have not been changed, the 'programme' remains the same.

To change the files in your computer you need to start to create positive images in your conscious mind. Build pictures of the good things that you desire. Get emotionally involved in the realisation of your goal. Design the person that you need to become and then design an action plan to become that person. Start to expect the good things that you desire. When you expect things to happen, they usually do.

You have now engaged in the process of transferring the images you have created into your sub-conscious mind. The programme is being changed. The files are being replaced and guess what? Your results will change. Why?

Because your sub-conscious mind cannot reject or accept ideas, it can only do what it is programmed to do.

When I understood this idea, my life changed because what is even more amazing is that when you have decided what you really, really want – your sub-conscious mind will find ways of bringing about your goal. So focus on the What, not the How. Your Powerhouse will take care of that. 〞

Most of the skill of coaching lies in effective questioning, active listening and adopting a non-judgmental, non-directive stance. Coaches aren't there to tell or advise their clients what to do; their role is simply to guide, challenge and support them in finding their own answers.

That's one of the reasons why coaching works – it is founded on the premise that individuals must make their own decisions and take responsibility for their own actions and their own happiness and fulfillment. If coaching 'fails' (which is rare) it is usually because the individual being coached doesn't really want to change.

## The Wheel of Life

One of the most common questions people ask about coaching is 'How do you know where to start?' What they generally mean by this is that they recognize that they are dissatisfied and need to make changes to their lives, but there are so many areas of unhappiness or dissatisfaction that they don't know which to start with!

The most effective way a coach can help a client decide where their problems lie and set some priorities in dealing with them is to ask them to complete a *Wheel of Life*. This simple exercise enables the individual to examine the most significant areas in their life, and to assess how balanced the areas are and how happy and satisfied they feel about each.

> Great thoughts reduced to practice become great acts. **WILLIAM HAZLITT**

From this it becomes obvious which areas are most in need of attention and those which can help improve life balance.

## Goal setting

Perhaps one of the most vital aspects of coaching and one which trainee coaches can struggle with as they start to practise, is helping their clients to set goals. In order to be effective, goals must be SMART (Specific, Measurable, Agreed, Realistic and Time-bound). SMART goals are essential for enabling both the coach and the client to focus on *precisely* what the client wants to achieve.

If a goal is SPECIFIC it means that both the client and the coach are clear about exactly what achieving the goal entails. For example, 'My goal is to weigh nine stones by Christmas this year' is clear and specific, whereas 'My goal is to lose some weight', is not.

It is important that the goal is MEASURABLE in order to be able to assess whether what the client achieves is what they had originally intended. For example, 'My goal is to become more confident', is very difficult to measure. However, 'My goal is become sufficiently confident to go on holiday by myself by next summer' is very measurable.

If the client has AGREED to the goal, then they have taken ownership of it and have acknowledged that they are committed to taking the action necessary in order to achieve the goal.

If a goal is REALISTIC then it is, by definition, achievable, if not, there is no point the client trying to achieve it. Again, a goal that says 'My goal is to weigh nine stones by Christmas' if it's now the end of October and you currently weigh 18 stones, clearly is not a realistic goal!

The issue of TIME is also vital for the client and coach to be able to decide whether or not the goal has been achieved (otherwise it simply becomes a case of 'I haven't achieved it *yet*'). Similarly, setting a time frame provides motivation for the client and a framework within which to act – e.g. 'Working backwards from that date, I can see exactly what I need to do and when in order to achieve my goal.'

The TGROW model, SMART goals, spiritual coaching, values, questioning … the residential training weekend is packed full of new and challenging information and for many the Saturday night is just as long and spiritual (in a different sort of way!) as the two days it intercepts.

One of the main, but 'untaught' new experiences that the majority of people take away with them is an absolute feeling of camaraderie, friendship and shared purpose. They may have been keen and potentially very dedicated before the two days but by Sunday night, inspired by the enthusiasm of the trainers … they're off, and flying!

At the end of the course, students are asked to complete a feedback form in the interests of quality control and continuous improvement. No matter how apprehensive or unsure they were at 9am on Saturday morning, these are just an indication of the sort of comments that invariably are the norm:

> Where did the time go? Not once did I look at my watch or say to myself 'Can't wait for lunch'! I came away inspired, challenged but feeling supported and eager to get going.   LINDA WATSON

> The course has equipped me with the skills to coach at an outstanding level; the support that you receive during your training is unmatched.   KAY GIRE

> This was a fantastic first step of the life coaching journey filled with passion, leading by example and supporting us as we change and grow to become the best.   LESLEY READER

> The weekend was thought provoking, spiritually lifting and of course challenging. A wonderful experience – more than I thought it would be. I hope I have taken it all in and look forward to being what I want to be.   CHRISTIAN SIMPSON

Whoever acquires knowledge but does not practice it is like one who ploughs a field but does not sow it.   ANON

# 5 A journey of ten thousand miles...

> Personally, I'm always ready to learn, although I do not always like being taught.
>
> WINSTON CHURCHILL

FOR MANY students, the reality of what they have committed to really hits home when they leave the residential weekend and are faced with the next step – starting to work towards accreditation.

Because of the amount of work that is required, including a certain number of hours of practical coaching, the minimum time in which the course can be completed is around three months. Some do it in this time, some take much longer. However, no matter if the weeks stretch into many, many months, the mentor coaches and other support staff are flexible, understanding and endlessly encouraging. It makes students *want* to succeed.

So the initial training weekend was great, and the vision of being a coach is so strong and tangible as to be a complete distraction, but… reality being what it is, students emerging from the residential course on the Sunday evening come down to earth with a bump on Monday morning – faced with resuming real life. However, theirs is a life now made even more challenging by 20 emails from Pam Stokes, Head of Distance Learning outlining what they need to do next.

If there's one person at Rivas Palmer who really has her finger on the pulse of what it's all about, it has to be Pam. She oversees the course-work, supervises the mentoring and monitors the content and standard of all aspects of the course. Most important for some, she has the final say on whether or not students pass the practical coaching assessment… a very important person indeed!

Pam is calm, patient, and has a wry sense of humour which combines with a friendly and highly approachable manner to make her a fantastic role model for aspiring coaches. Her feedback is always constructive and helpful, though always sufficiently challenging to ensure that students learn and are forced to push themselves that 'extra mile'.

Here Pam describes how she became involved in setting up Rivas Palmer and the challenges she and the trainee coaches face on their journey towards accreditation:

# We wanted to do much more than just run training courses

PAM STOKES | **66** I have known Natasha since the days pre-Rivas Palmer when we were both training.

After qualifying, I made a start building a life coaching business and met Natasha professionally on a few occasions. When she told me about her exciting new plans to start a coach training organisation and asked me if I would like to be Head of Distance Learning at Rivas Palmer, I jumped at the chance. I soon found myself agreeing to write the words for a brochure, and my husband Peter was only too happy to design the website with me providing the words.

Designing the business model wasn't a problem, but we wanted to do much more than just run training courses. Our own experience of coach training had shown us that what was really important was the issue of ongoing support and assistance, not just leaving people alone to flounder and become disillusioned once they had finished the residential training. We wanted to make sure we would always be there for everyone to ensure that they completed the course, and that we made it as straightforward as possible for them along the way.

### Our aim is to be challenging but to make everything as easy as possible

The format and content of the residential weekend has always been successful, so although there have been changes in trainers and the content of some sessions, it has essentially remained the same. However, we have continuously tweaked the distance learning pack – in response to feedback from students and mentors. Our aim overall is to make everything as easy to understand as possible.

No matter how hard you try to think things through and cancel out all complexities and potential sources of confusion, there are occasions when someone responds in a way you didn't expect them to. If it's just a one-off that's okay, you can simply talk through the misunderstanding with them and point them in the right direction; however if a number of people are struggling with something then I will go back to address the problem and make changes to ensure it's clearer and easier to understand

Distance learning inevitably means that a lot of work is computer based and people who have little computer experience can struggle, simply because the whole business of typing work and responding to emails can be much more complex and challenging for them because of the unfamiliarity with the process. Out of all of our learners there are only one or two students who haven't got computers and/or haven't had email addresses. We have advised them to get help setting up email addresses by going to their local college or library, or maybe getting a friend to help them. Downloading emails at the library is certainly a lot easier these days than it was even a year ago.

The Assessment Questions are designed to cover everything students have learned on the course and are also set to cover the OCN (Open College Network) requirements. The questions have evolved to ensure that they were more closely in line with these.

The Assignment Questions were pretty straightforward to come up with as they basically follow the two reasons why people want to train to be a coach: to take coaching back to the work place, or to set up a coaching practice.

### The perils of the practical work

The practice coaching sessions with mentors are often quite challenging for students although they do give very positive feedback on what they get out of them. Courses without support and practical guidance may mean the experience may be more comfortable for students but then they don't learn and move ahead and that would be as frustrating for us as we know it would be for them.

In respect of the final practical assessment of coaching, no one has actually failed though a number have been asked to do it again. Poor performance can often be down to nerves and on rare occasions I might ask a student if they would like to do it again if I feel they hadn't shown their true capabilities.

Students are asked to have practice clients and to submit notes on their sessions, as part of the accreditation process. The parts of the practical coaching people tend to struggle with the most are distinguishing between getting the client to set a goal and set an outcome for the session. Also the questioning process; students can fail to ask open questions or they can ask quite superficial questions which can often mean they are following their own agenda.

When this happens the client can be led down a certain path which doesn't bear much relation to their needs. Those being coached will usually go along with it, but at the end of the session they will feel dissatisfied and this will be reflected in the feedback they give. Often the students themselves also feel they haven't done well in these circumstances, but can't see why. For this reason I ask students to send reports of their first couple of practice coaching sessions at the outset rather than saving them all up to the end.

I now also ask them to report on what questions they asked, so I can spot exactly why things might not be going as well as they would like and can pinpoint ways of helping them to put matters right before they do all the sessions and it's too late. Once they have submitted all of the required number of sessions which is currently a total of 12 (3 clients × 4 sessions each) they are assessed and feedback is provided. This can sometimes mean me giving up to three pages of feedback to some students, though it's worth it. It really helps build their confidence and move them forward.

### Learning and commitment

Feedback is a necessary part of the learning process whether for practical or written work and it's given to students in the form of a sandwich so their achievements are recognised as well as areas they need to develop. Occasionally it's a problem for some people because they perceive any feedback to be criticism. Often talking it through with that person will result in them realising that in fact it is something that happens in all areas of their lives, which can then lead them to consider having coaching for themselves. On the whole though, people appreciate the feedback and say how helpful it's been in their learning journey.

On our courses, we haven't found it makes any difference whether students are 'academic' or not. Generally we don't mark spelling, grammar or sentence construction – so none of those things are differentiators, though I would comment if work was so badly written that it is difficult to read, as then I feel that this probably would have some impact on their future dealings with clients.

The only real thing that differentiates students is their commitment to completing the course. Those who are really committed will do it no matter what occurs along the way, and some of our students have faced some real disasters during their training including illness, bereavement, redundancy or divorce. In these cases, if we don't hear from someone for a while we will make contact just to see that they are alright and to reassure them that they are welcome to return to their studies whenever they are ready.

However, some others just find that they are too busy or lack sufficient commitment to make the time. Overall there have only been about ten who have withdrawn from the course completely – one or two because they have just wanted to experience the residential weekend as a personal learning journey and haven't wanted to achieve the accreditation. This is something which our new modular system addresses.

### A perfect daily challenge

Being Head of Distance Learning at Rivas Palmer has changed my life by bringing together all the things I feel I'm good at and enjoy doing. I have a very logical side to me but also a people side and this is the perfect 50/50 combination. I have gone from a situation a few years ago where I was gradually building up a coaching practice, to a situation where I am constantly busy all the time with work mapped out ahead of me for as far as I can see.

My challenge now is very much to control my workload! Most of the time keeping motivated is no problem as I feel completely immersed and enthusiastic about what I'm doing. Of course, the job is demanding but in some ways it's easy too, I guess because I've created the work and I know what's involved, what the answers are and what I have to do. Just dealing with it all is a challenge sometimes though, and I have to consciously strive to maintain a balanced life and make time for me.

Coaching is great because you never stop learning, which for me means I never get bored. I consistently learn a lot from the assessments I do and will often be impressed by a student asking a really good, searching question during the session – I make a mental note to remember what it is and use it myself! As a result, I think my own coaching has definitely improved and my enjoyment of coaching is ever increasing. **99**

This book, for obvious reasons, focuses a great deal on the coach training programme provided by Rivas Palmer, but of course, there are many other training organisations in the market. This competition is viewed as *a good thing*; it provides impetus to Rivas Palmer to consistently strive for excellence and quality and to ensure high levels of customer (student) satisfaction.

> All good things come to those who wait, but only what's left behind by those who seized the opportunities. **ABRAHAM LINCOLN**

In fact it is heartening and reassuring that the majority of students who commit to Rivas Palmer's coach training only do so after a considerable amount of research into what other courses have to offer:

## Thought-provoking and powerful training

**PAUL STONEHOUSE** | 66 I chose Rivas Palmer from many coach training organisations for several reasons, the main ones being the practical nature of the programme, the support provided during and after training, and the emphasis on developing spiritual coaching.

I found their course training days thought-provoking and powerful, and the support through the qualification process prompt, helpful and insightful. The written and practical work required for qualification was very relevant to what I wanted to develop. Having recently qualified, that support is still there when required which I find enormously reassuring as I build my new practice. 99

Anyone who has studied the process of 'learning' will know that not only do people learn in different ways but their commitment and motivation can vary widely depending on personality, circumstance and methods of stimulus. However, Rivas Palmer's commitment to ensuring that *all* their students 'get there in the end' is paramount, and certainly those who are straggling can expect an understanding attitude from their mentor coaches, as this mentor coach explains:

## Timing is everything

**BELINDA MOLLROSS** | 66 There's a difference between external stimulation (which is what happens to people on the residential weekend and which doesn't actually come from within), and internal motivation and commitment. Students get buzzed up on the residential weekends and then come

Monday, they have to go back to real life and work and it all starts to fall away.

A student's own reality and their ability to crack the training is a lot to do with timing. Some people jump in with two feet and get on with it; I've had students who are on the phone on Monday, raring to go. And that's great, I can see that they've got the momentum they need.

A lot of what happens in training seminars and workshops is external stimulation – and of course once that's gone, you've got to motivate yourself. If the initial introduction to the training hasn't really and truly hit a button that has opened some sort of awareness in yourself, you're going to have difficulty sustaining the momentum.

Timing is everything. For many people what can happen is that they'll do the work at a slow and steady pace, so change doesn't always happen immediately. It may be 12 to 24 months before it actually all comes together. When you proceed at your own pace there's no right or wrong, it's what's appropriate for you.

And not everybody that's on a course is going to be at the same place timing-wise when they do it, all sorts of things may be getting in the way. But if it is the right time, it will just flow, it will work.

However, next to timing is commitment – the idea of something sounds really good, but actually doing it...? Well let's just say that I like the idea of a clean flat, but I don't like doing the housework!

You have to find what the trigger is within yourself, and what you respond to. For example, a lot of people leave things to the eleventh hour and will only do them then. There's something about that pressure that will make them perform – they say they hate it, but they actually construct events that way.

So, when it comes to designing a training course and the associated support, you have to take these people into account also. You may not agree with the approach, but for them that's how it works. Who are we to say what's right? 🔊

The training may be a challenge, may be taxing, time-consuming and downright terrifying at times, but looking back most people find it an exhilarating and life-enhancing experience. Okay, maybe they wouldn't want to do it again, but otherwise...

## Leap before you look

JOHN BLAKEY

The steps that freeze us,
The illusion of barbed wire,
The sheer agony of becoming who we are,
Like a yawn, a stretch, a chasm,
You stare into the abyss of freedom,
And it stares into you,
Side by side,
With the birds on the runway,
Waiting for something to happen,
Forever watching a looping film,
Waiting for it to come to us,
We pray for the courage to take a tiny step,
We pray for the fresh air of liberation,
We pray for support and strength and grace,
As into an open future we fall.

You cannot discover new oceans unless
you lose sight of the shore.　　FRANCIS DRAKE

# 6 Starting to coach other people

> Silence is the element in which great things
> fashion themselves together. **THOMAS CARLYLE**

HEARING, READING about and discussing coaching is all very well, but it's a bit like preparing for a parachute jump. All good stuff until suddenly – crunch time – your bluff is called and you actually have to *do it*.

Some practice coaching sessions are held on the residential training weekend, but at that stage, as you only have to coach similarly nervous and inexperienced fellow trainees, it all seems more possible. It's when you're on your own and facing coaching real people who perhaps don't know or understand much about coaching or what you're trying to achieve, that it all suddenly becomes very challenging…

As James A Belasco says in his foreword to *Coaching for Leadership* –

*'Coaching is not a spectator sport. A productive coaching relationship begins with two people with fires in their bellies: one who wants desperately to move forward and another who yearns to help that person make the journey.*

*To be coached successfully you must want – desperately – to move, to learn, to grow and you must be truly dedicated to spend the time and energy to do so. Coaching isn't something that happens to you; it happens through you. As a person being coached you must be an active player in the game, not a spectator in the second row.'*

The Rivas Palmer coaching programme requires the trainee to complete and record 12 practice client sessions. And of course, these 12 sessions have to be of a quality worth writing up, which means many, many more sessions with willing guinea pig clients.

Frankly, the first one is like jumping off the top diving board when you know you can't swim, have a fear of heights and suffer an inherent and irreversible lack of coordination. Scary! And not only do you have to coach practice clients, you have to find them. Most people rope in friends, relatives, workmates, and neighbours. Good in some ways, but in others it can make the difficult even harder. As many soon discover it can be:

- Easier to coach strangers
- Easier to coach on the telephone
- Easier to imagine chewing on broken glass than to contemplate not only convincing a total stranger to be coached but also proving in practice that you can do it!

## There's no 'i' in coach

The most difficult thing about coaching is that as the coach you have to forget about yourself. This is in contrast to normal life where usually we are having a conversation exactly because of who we are. We are a friend, neighbour, colleague, family member, partner – whatever our role, someone is talking to us and telling us things because of this.

They want us to listen, to be supportive in an unquestioning sort of a way, to accept what they have done, to tell them it will all be alright and that we still cherish and respect them, and to tell them what to do based on our experience.

Coaching conversations are different. Coaching is all about the person being coached and very little to do with the coach. The coach is a facilitator, an interrogator, and a catalyst for helping their client think about their life and see their situation – and sometimes the world – in a different way.

> I keep six honest serving men.
> (They taught me all I knew);
> Their names are What and Why and When
> And How and Where and Who.
>
> **RUDYARD KIPLING**

Coaching questions are open questions. For anyone not familiar with the concept of open questions, they're the ones which can't be answered with a 'yes' or 'no' and those which don't lead or direct the person being questioned to answer in a certain way (Fans of TV courtroom dramas will be familiar with the concept!).

Really great coaching questions are those that seem to stop the world for the person being coached and really make them look at things differently. Often their answer will be preceded by the phrase 'You know, I've never thought of it like that before ...'. Eureka! A breakthrough – the client has had a 'lightbulb' moment – that's what great coaching questions are all about.

# Practice clients haven't been on the course and don't know the rules!

KATIE DAY | **66** The worst aspect of training is when you start with your practice clients and suddenly realise they haven't been on the course and don't know the rules!! Aaargh!

You have your model all laid out in front of you, your open questions and a watch to keep time, and they go off on a tangent, don't stick to the timetable, start wandering, don't know what they want to achieve, want you to fix it for them and generally misbehave quite appallingly!! But hey, I love them all the more for it – there are never obstacles or problems in life, only opportunities for learning and growth! Now where did I hear that? **99**

Normally, when we talk to people we have our own agenda. We have opinions, we have moods, we like to relate what is being said to our own values, standards and experiences. Even those who appear to demonstrate little in the way of ego are running what they are being told past an internal screening system which says: 'How do I feel about that?' 'Is what they are saying right or wrong?' 'Have I had a similar experience?' 'Based on my knowledge, what do I think is going to happen to them?' 'Are they doing what I feel to be correct?' 'What does this mean for me?'

You get the picture. There are a whole battalion of other filters, but what they all have in common is the ME word. Even the most unselfish and caring of us always ultimately and unconsciously focus on ourselves.

## The power of active listening

Everything changes in coaching. The trainee coach is introduced to *active listening* which means completely forgetting about oneself and shifting your entire focus to the client.

Ideally, each coaching session should be made up of 30% questioning and 70% listening. This is to enable the client to have time to fully consider every question they are asked and to have an opportunity to form links between their current situation and the range of options that may be open to them if they want to change.

Concentrating on actively listening enables the coach to focus 100% on the client rather than being involved in their own thought processes and what questions they should be asking next. At the start of their practice coaching sessions, most trainee coaches worry that sensible and pertinent questions won't come and indeed, some do initially find that they are hesitant and the process is somewhat disjointed.

But over time and with experience, by practising listening and immersing oneself in the coaching conversation, it all starts to come naturally – and 'the right questions' just start to flow.

In active listening the coach focuses on a number of significant areas, for example:

- What the client doesn't say as well as what they do say – this can indicate a great deal about their feelings and perceptions and also that they might be saying what they think you want to hear.
- The actual words they use – in Neuro-Linguistic Programming terminology, these can indicate the filters they generally use to monitor the world around them.
- What role they are accustomed to playing in life – the phraseology they use may show whether they primarily act as a parent, child, teacher, etc.
- The way in which they say things, for example, happy, depressed, angry, tearful, apologetic – this often reveals far more about the client's true feelings than the words they use.
- Repetition of certain words, facts, or even expressions – these can demonstrate an individual's values and beliefs or show how they customarily behave in certain situations.

Here Susie Fletcher, ex-nurse and Rivas Palmer accredited coach comments on her experiences:

## I felt so energised that I danced around the kitchen

SUSIE FLETCHER

**66** After the high of the residential weekend, when life was never to be the same again, the realisation set in – I have got to start to coach someone! Well – the safest people were obviously my study buddies and friends I had met on the course; I didn't have to convince them that coaching worked – they knew that already.

So, I duly bought a coaching diary and started to make appointments with them. We started by being professional, but sometimes hilarity crept in as we nervously attempted to coach each other. There were also the odd uneasy moments when we worried whether our darkest secrets would remain confidential between us or would find their way back to those at the top – showing us to have huge issues and anxieties. What a worry – could we ever be coaches with all these issues to deal with?

For my first few sessions I would have a copy of *'Effective Coaching'* lying open on the desk, or Laura Berman Fortgang's list of Wisdom

Access questions and the very helpful list of questions from the Rivas Palmer manual. Although I'd feverishly mug up on a few questions, alas they never seemed relevant at the time and I could hardly stop and search for the right one while my clients waited!

In the beginning, it all seemed very difficult as we practised our TGROW model on each other

… struggling with the difference between outcomes and goals

…and whether we were asking open questions or closed,

… and how to get past the Reality stage when there were already 40 minutes on the clock

…to battle through to the end of each session and the magical words,

'So on a score of 0–10 how committed are you to taking this action?'

Slowly, week by week, we began to see progress – last week I got my client to set a goal, and this week we didn't spend so long in reality before running out of time, and today – hurrah we did it all in 45 minutes and I got good feedback – only two closed questions!

We learnt to give each other gentle feedback and made a pact with each other that nothing was meant 'personally', it was just constructive feedback on the coaching. For me there were so many habits to unlearn. I came from a background of nursing where it was fairly normal to give advice and even unasked–for advice!

Making assumptions was another habit – based on anticipating patients' needs especially when frail in health and elderly and even deciphering what they were communicating. So I had to learn to listen patiently until the 'client' had stopped talking and then ask a relevant question and learn NOT to be too helpful!

Then that magical day came when we reached the end of a session and I realised that I hadn't thought once about how I was doing because I had been so immersed in my client, who had just made a huge breakthrough!

I felt so energised after the call that I danced around the kitchen.

After this, I began to spread my wings and try out this new skill on other people. I started on my family, practising the skills only to be greeted with – 'Mum, you're coaching me again!'

My son had spread the word amongst his friends and one of the girls who had had counselling wanted to see how coaching worked and volunteered to be a practice client. She was great as she was very goal orientated which I found helpful. This was such a new concept to me, as I had not consciously set any goals up to that point. I still remember one of the trainers saying on the residential weekend – 'A person without goals is a mindless generality' – I sat in shock for at least half an hour!

Comparing notes with coaching buddies was sometimes useful and sometimes demoralising because inevitably some people grasped the coaching principles quicker and people progressed at different rates. Human nature prevails and we judge ourselves more firmly than we would dream of doing to others.

I knew for me it was important to learn by applying the practical side of things before attempting the written work, which then began to make sense. It was like learning a new language with a different vocabulary. Things like 'self-limiting beliefs' and 'values' and 'goal setting' didn't feature much in the clinic room when giving childhood immunisations or changing a dressing.

It was all moving ahead but nevertheless, there were days when nothing made sense and I would feel like giving it all up. Then I would ring up my mentor coach and talk it over, or phone Pam Stokes, feeling rather foolish, and she always seemed to make it clear. Always having someone to refer back to was fantastic – the level of support was excellent. 99

## Listen, don't judge

A key component of coaching is suspending one's natural tendency to be judgmental. Normally, even the nicest and kindest of people amongst us continuously assesses other people according to our own values and beliefs – which may have absolutely no relevance to those whom we are judging.

But by judging people, particularly in a coaching relationship, we are preventing them from identifying and pursuing their own best course of action and their own most beneficial path. We may also make them afraid of exploring and visualising the person they might wish to become because they fear we might judge them on that also.

Additionally, as coaches we also run the risk of making them feel inadequate, defensive, guilty, unworthy or even downright angry! This will destroy their feelings of self-worth and lower their feelings of self-esteem, let alone the rapport between us – exactly opposite to the benefits coaching should achieve!

The ultimate effect of being judgmental is that our client will be unwilling to communicate openly about their thoughts and feelings and may not even be able to think clearly about what they want to achieve and how to go about it.

> Training to be a coach is like training a dog. You just have to keep on doing what you know you have to do over and over and over and over again, without letting up. You have to change your behaviour until it becomes second nature to do things in a certain way and you stop consciously having to think about it. You have to work together with your client. You have to bond. Then you have to start to relax and enjoy the situation, really tune in to a new way of communicating – coach and client working together. That's when it all starts to hum.

## Different clients move at different speeds

GINNY COLWELL

**66** I have had some wonderful ah-ha! moments with clients. When you really feel that you have helped them to realise a whole new range of possibilities, it is like an energy channel is released. Having been stuck, they are suddenly up and running and you can see their whole bodies lighten up.

You have to accept that different clients move at different speeds and not judge them as to how quickly they progress. The important thing is that they feel they are moving forward.

I had one client who I didn't feel I was helping at all and after the third session, I thought that I really needed some feedback and expected him to be a bit negative about the experience. When I asked him how he thought the coaching was going his reply was 'Fantastic, it has really moved me on.' It was a good lesson for me. **99**

As coaching is all about the other person and their development, the coach's beliefs, attitudes and experiences have absolutely nothing at all to do with the process and at no stage are they relevant. Being judgmental precludes establishing empathy, trust and openness with clients – all of which are vital to a productive and successful coaching relationship.

## The best coaching sessions are those when the coach says hardly anything

CATHERINE STRATTA

66 Suspending judgement is hard to do, but once mastered it is a wonderful tool. Questions usually occur to the coach from the client's words. Often the best coaching sessions are those when the coach says hardly anything, as then the onus is on the client. Questions must be open, and should help to move the client onwards. Listening is a key skill for a coach, and it is important to know when to hold a silence, so that the client has time to think.

I have found that often after there has been quite a long silence the client has had a light bulb moment (i.e. a moment when they realise something about themselves or their situation that they were previously unaware of). For coaching to be effective it is important that the client is in charge of the session; theirs is the agenda and the coach steers with questions, but only in the direction provided by the client. This is a true designed alliance. 99

For many students, their first port of call for practice clients is their study buddy, and if they're lucky, they have more than one. Once you've got over the initial first few practice sessions and move on to coaching 'real people', your buddies can still be a tremendous help and support in keeping you going, reassuring you, giving you confidence, and if necessary, providing a shoulder to cry on.

Here three study buddies recount how it's worked for them…

## The best of buddies

YAMIE BOAKES

66 Over our residential weekend, we were lucky to find that at least five of us lived within five miles of each other. This lead to emails flying to arrange to meet up and practise some of the skills that we had learnt.

The first couple of sessions we coached each other to gain confidence in ourselves and our abilities. Later, we would talk about how our practice client sessions were going, discuss issues and give each other the reassurance and motivation to continue with the coursework.

Whatever situation came up, someone had either experienced it or would suggest a solution. We were all in the same boat. We weren't judgmental of each other – just supportive. 99

**SUE MARCHANT**

❝ Working full time and having a young family, it would have been easy to give in when the going got tough and when I got to August and realised I was struggling, I nearly did.

Little did I know at the start of the residential weekend that I would come away from it having met three people who were not only going to be my study buddies but ultimately my best friends and business partners as well!

We met monthly for three or four hours and took it in turns to talk about how we had got on in the previous month: our successes, errors and fears. Here I realised that no matter what our own individual circumstances, we all went through and experienced the same emotions and the way to get over them was to listen to other's experiences and get on with it. I had some fantastic support from my husband and mentor, but what the group added was the 'something extra' that only those who were currently going through the course could provide.

I am quite a competitive person, but what inspired me within our group was the lack of individual competitiveness and the teamwork we displayed to reach the winning post – it was not about finishing first but getting to the finish line together. When any one of us got their results, it was as much a delight as receiving our own.

We are all very different, but what we were able to do was use each other's strengths to help us grow. In short – we walked the talk!

I have no doubts that I could have completed the course – a year or two down the line… but without the other three it would have been twice as demanding and not half as much fun. ❞

**CLAIRE ELSTON**

❝ How wrong was I when I thought that Rivas Palmer were shirking their promises of support throughout the accreditation process when they encouraged us, as new students, to 'buddy up'. It was, in hindsight, a clever ploy enabling students to get maximum levels of support from each other as well as from head office.

My initial study buddy lived in West London, and we had exchanged a couple of telephone calls and e-mails when she told me that she had met up with several other students living nearby. The meeting had been useful and they were intending to meet on a regular basis with each buddy hosting a meeting at their home.

Until then, I was not really achieving very much on my own. Having given up my job to study full time, I was feeling lonely too. This called for action; I e-mailed the group and asked if I could join. The prospect of working with others and sharing experiences made the three hour round trip more than worthwhile.

We met monthly and practised coaching each other, as well as each giving updates on our learning and progress throughout the month. Strangely enough we found that we were all experiencing the same problems at the same time! This gave us the opportunity to work through solutions together, achieving fantastic results.

I have now finished the course achieving a distinction, and owe it largely to the support and encouragement of my study buddies and Rivas Palmer 99

## Using coaching skills in everyday life

One of the great benefits of coach training is that it teaches you the value of listening and actively questioning in every aspect of normal life so that you get the other person's viewpoint before you leap in with your own. In both personal and business situations this can be a great advantage. When you feel you have questioned and listened to people and understand their situation, you are in a much stronger position to match your position with theirs. This doesn't mean becoming obsequious or a 'yes' person, but it certainly can cut down on conflict, misunderstanding or disappointment.

> Any joy and exuberance we experience in living are the fruits of our willingness to risk, our openness to change and our ability to create what we want for our lives.
>
> **DAVID MCNALLY**

For example, coaching can be remarkably effective in sales and this is borne out by some of the most effective sales training programmes – they're not called 'coaching' but their approach is very similar.

Basically, if you're trying to sell, don't plough right in there and *tell* your prospective customer about what you're selling and why they need it. Develop rapport, *ask* them about their problems and what they feel would solve them. If you're lucky (and skilled), what they are seeking is what you've got, and you'll be well placed to match the benefits of your product or service with what they have already told you are their wants and needs.

## The joy of coaching

So as their skills develop and emerge through practice sessions, coaching starts to become real to trainees and as it does, it becomes more and more emotive. It stops becoming a seemingly insurmountable challenge and becomes what it will remain – moving, rewarding, enthralling and exhilarating. Up to now, we've wondered if we will ever reach the stage of experiencing these emotions with clients, but now we start to and it's GREAT!

## What I love about coaching

VANESSA WESTWELL

66 I love the moment when I ask a question and there is a long, long pause. Over the silence of the telephone line I can hear the client's mind working. The apparent lull in the session is actually charged with energy and mounting excitement, as I know they are having a breakthrough in their thinking.

These are the 'Aha!' moments that help my clients to move ahead in leaps, to leave their fears behind, or to see through a limiting belief that has been nagging at them for years.

These are the moments in coaching that make it all worthwhile. 99

> Your dreams tell you what to do; your reason tells you how to do it. JONAS SALK

VANESSA WESTWELL

**66** This is a poem I wrote after a particularly poignant coaching session. It is an attempt to describe some of the excitement and wonder I feel as a coach. Sometimes when I see my client experience a breakthrough in their thinking, it seems that coaching is the finest and most rewarding profession in the world. **99**

## When I helped her...

When I helped her

When I held the space

When I listened

Transfixed

And gently

Watched

Her face transformed

Before my eyes.

At first

Tremulous, scattered energies

Tumbled anxiously

Her eyes held fear

And wariness

Yet also hope

Hope that I could help

Hope that she would find an answer

And she did.

# 7 Walking the talk

> Here is the test to find whether your mission
> on earth is finished. If you're alive, it isn't.
>
> RICHARD BACH

ONE OF the big and sometimes confusing dilemmas for trainee coaches is being told that coaches 'don't need to be perfect', yet also being told how important it is to 'walk the talk'. It's like a big scary sandwich with Snow White on one side, the Wicked Witch on the other, and the wide-eyed coach stuck in between!

But coaches aren't perfect, they don't lead – and usually don't aspire to lead – perfect lives, and in fact, often have more chaotic and angst-ridden lives than many. So what? As long as they conduct themselves professionally, it doesn't matter. The coaching relationship isn't about *their* life; it's all about their clients'.

Okay, so what's all this 'walk the talk' business then if coaching doesn't mean having a perfect, trouble-free life?

Basically what it means is having a positive mental attitude, aligning your life with your values and believing that it is both possible and desirable to change. A positive mental attitude means looking for and recognising the good that either exists or may be derived from even the worst situation. Taking this approach habitually means that every problem is perceived as a challenge and an opportunity rather than an unchangeable negative event.

Studies have shown that people are drawn to those with a positive mental attitude. So, by consciously adopting and continually reinforcing a positive mental attitude, the whole demeanour of a coach becomes 'attract-ive' to others, including prospective clients.

On the reverse side, no potential client is going to want to be coached by someone who seems negative, pessimistic or despondent. It just doesn't add up!

Spirituality and values are key – and interlinked – aspects of 'walking the talk' and essential elements of effective coaching. So helping a client identify their true values is critical. It involves asking them to list what principles or feelings are really important to them in life, then comparing each one against the others until they have established their relative importance.

By going through this sometimes lengthy process, clients often come to realize that things they thought they valued highly are actually not very important, or may not represent their true feelings at all. Likewise, they currently may not be giving sufficient attention to things that they actually care about very deeply, and this can be causing them stress, discomfort or pain. Focusing on values can be an excellent way of getting to the heart of what a client wants and needs to achieve, regardless of the type of issue involved.

> The danger with a lot of positive thinking training is that some people can become unbearably and unrealistically positive – so heavenly that they are no earthly good.
>
> **RICHARD DENNY**

As mentioned earlier in the book, religion or spirituality of any type or denomination need not, and should not, provide any barrier to effective coaching as long as the client can accept the concept of free will and their own responsibility for choices, actions and happiness. In the context of coaching, 'spirituality' means understanding who you are, what your purpose is and what you stand for. There are many different contexts in which this can apply.

## Do we really know what 'spirituality' means?

**MEERA VOHORA**

66 'Spirituality' is very chic at the moment and sometimes can be a distraction to discovering our authentic self. There is also a huge confusion between religion and spirituality, because it seems that being spiritual, and not religious, is the 'in' thing now. But 'spiritual' is kind of like the word 'love' – it's used a lot, but what are we really saying?

As a recently qualified life coach, I hear many people, both in the workplace and personally, talking about searching for 'something more'. People say, 'I'd just like to become more spiritual as a person.' As a result, the UK in particular has seen a rise in the popularity of yoga because it helps to cope with stress, and meditation which helps clear the mind, plus all the rest, t'ai chi, philosophy, reiki, etc.

One need only look at the many books on this subject to see it's a hot topic. But these are merely 'tools' to help us achieve that bigger picture. We need to stop and ask ourselves, what do we actually mean when we say we want to be 'spiritual' and what is the bigger picture?

Let's look deeper into what we mean by spirituality. To begin with

I've discovered that I really associate spirituality with inspiration. When I see a person, a sunset, a work of art, a movie, or read a story that touches me, that gives me new hope and new life, and whatever it was that moved me becomes spiritual in a sense. This is because the word 'inspire' means to take new breath, into the body; 'spirit' and 'inspiration' have the same root.

But spirituality can also mean something else. It reminds us that there is something else 'out there', something more than our everyday existence that we can reach out to, and hope for.

In essence, spirituality is the capacity to embody in our everyday lives qualities like love, a sense of humour, friendliness, wisdom, and the courage to do the right thing. Spirituality reminds us that we are connected to one another. That we are not isolated individuals, here only for our own happiness and gratification. The 'contribution' element of a spiritual life is based in the belief that, in order to receive fulfilment, you need to give. It focuses on how an individual can contribute to the 'greater good' in some way.

Spiritual coaching develops a client's desire to achieve absolute equilibrium between material, and giving and sharing goals. Some examples that actively demonstrate this are conservation projects, humanitarian work, or social education, to name but a few.

So spiritual coaching is about 'being' the person who is able to 'do'. It's about creating the right, positive mental framework. When you can visualise achieving your goal, you achieve it a lot faster and more effectively. With spirituality, we are striving for that bigger picture; a full and all inclusive-awareness which some choose to call enlightenment or nirvana

As Nelson Mandela said: 'We are free, to be free.' **❯❯**

Focusing on one's own values and their importance and trying to live a life in alignment with those values often means having to question the meaning and purpose of life, which in career terms can often have a very dramatic impact.

Many people start off on a career because they felt it was 'what was expected of them' or end up in a particular job because it was 'the best one offered to me at the time'. There are plenty more examples of how random our choices sometimes are, and just as many, equally significant stories about how what one *thought* had meaning and purpose, turned out not to be enough.

# A vehicle of service ... honouring those who choose to work with me

CATHERINE STRATTA

**❝** I believe that I am just starting on my true purpose in life. Originally, I went to Medical School and studied for four years before leaving because of various frustrations. I had rationalised my decision to myself (it was nearly 20 years ago now) but I see now that the main reason I left was because I wanted to spend more time with patients. I believed that talking to them and spending time with them was as important as giving drugs.

Unfortunately, at the time the medical profession and the NHS were undergoing substantial change. Gone were the days when you could wait in a surgery and the doctor would take time to see everyone – now there are surgery times and appointment 'slots' within which doctors are expected to operate. Looking back, I realise (with the help of a coaching mindset) that this was a violation of my values and was both frustrating and intolerable.

Ian Mcdermott (interview in Coach, 2003:32) states: *'For me coaching is a vehicle of service, one which enables me to honour those who choose to work with me.'* I can really identify with this, as it is exactly how I feel. I also believe that I will derive a great deal of satisfaction through seeing the transformation in people I coach. I have already seen this in practice clients, and know how wonderful it is to share in their joy when they become 'free' to realise their ambitions. With these thoughts in mind, I am eagerly anticipating starting a coaching practice.

I am very excited about the prospect of helping people from a coaching perspective and participating in such a dynamic relationship. It feels good to be able to put my people skills to the fore, and be able to work for myself in a creative way, and also to be able to realise one of the early ambitions I had on entering Medical School – to serve people and be able to really make a difference. **❞**

One of the great side effects of walking the talk, being spiritual and living in alignment with one's values is the amount of energy and passion it gives you for life in general. When compared to that dreadful, 'do I really have to?' sluggishness which results from a job you hate or a situation you're less than thrilled about, it's like constantly running on high-octane fuel! (Okay, not all the time, that debilitating gloom can still descend on even the most effervescent of coaches when faced with a huge stack of filing, or last week's ironing…)

For me, a definition of a happy life is when I wake up in the morning and can't wait to get started on the day ahead (and no, my middle name isn't Pollyanna). It certainly doesn't happen every day, but it's what I aspire to: fulfillment = motivation = joy!

> People are easily divided into two groups – the life-enhancers and the life drainers…
>
> AUTHOR SUSAN HILL WRITING ABOUT THE LATE
> DUKE OF DEVONSHIRE

## I have found my true internal motivation through coaching

JUSTINE WILKINSON

❝ Can you combine full-time University studying, coaching accreditation and starting to build a successful coaching practice? I decided this was something that I wanted to do and I enrolled in a BA Honours Counselling Studies degree course. I started University in September 2003 and attended my Rivas Palmer coaching course in October 2003. I am really pleased that I have chosen to do both and am 'loving' my life now.

I am passionate about what I am doing. It is stimulating, invigorating, enjoyable and empowering. My biggest challenge has been to apply realistic deadlines – and be prepared to review and extend them to allow for the usual unexpected interruptions! I have stopped being so hard on myself and in doing so, am achieving so much more.

I have not found conflict working in both counselling and coaching; in fact studying for my University modules has helped me to accelerate my own personal development. The tutors all have their areas of expertise and lecture on different theoretical approaches to psychology and 'helping'. The extensive University reading lists recommend many of the books on the coaching course list. I have found this stops me procrastinating, I do the reading now and expand it to a broader philosophical context.

It was a little daunting to be a 'fresher', lost around the campus, trying to find lecture rooms and get into a studying routine. However, I settled into University life very quickly, without the problems and social distractions many of my peers had to face. Several of my colleagues said to me 'How do you study full time, do your coaching and raise three young children? – You are so organised!'

Yes, I am, but I have lots of advantages – a nice home to come home to, food on the table, a place to work from, family support, and was not tempted by the social distractions!

By choosing to do both courses concurrently, I was able to retain a clear structure to my working week, lots of social interaction, intellectual stimulation, feedback on my work and time and space to gradually drop down a gear from my previous pace of working life, which met my own personal needs.

I have found my true internal motivation through the work that I do. I am able to satisfy my philosophical and academic interests in the existence, meaning, purpose and potential of individuals, while working towards a career where I can work collaboratively with clients to help them to find their own unique growth and positive gains.

### Choosing to have choices

To date, I have coached some wonderful clients. They have all worked so hard at their self-set goals and achieved so much. Two have made positive career changes; one – a very senior manager – asked her employer for flexible-working from home before agreeing to accept a new role. She told me, 'It's so obvious, but I never saw it. I now realise I never gave myself permission to leave the office on time and it was me, not my company that didn't allow me to have the work/home balance I craved!'

On reflection, I think I was very like her when I worked. If I had engaged a coach I could have seen I did have far more choice than my perception would allow at the time!

I have also coached one client through a business start up, which continues to go really well for him. It has helped me with lots of ideas for my own business!

The client outcome that I feel most personally satisfied with to date, was with a really fabulous person; a young housewife whose youngest child had started school. She was a really hard-working client and achieved her goals very quickly. As we came to the end of our contract, she told me that her personal results had really boosted her self-esteem and she felt for the first time in her life confident enough to explore re-training in a specific career area.

She asked if I could continue to work with her on this and I was happy to do so. She is now enrolled in an access course leading to university entrance, which will help her to achieve her long-term goal. She had always looked at the reasons not to do this before and was filled with doubts about her own ability.

I am so proud of her achievement and really pleased for her. She has enlisted the readily available help and support from her husband and family, which previously she had always assumed did not exist. She has blossomed, is much more self-confident, has a belief in herself and she 'glows' with purpose and self-belief. I feel very privileged that through coaching I helped her realise her dream, sooner rather than later.

A referral from this client has lead to my first paying client – so my advice to any new coaches out there is practise, practise, practise – and let the results you and your client achieve together speak for themselves.

Now I have finished my first academic year I feel that coaching came into my life at the right time for me. I was ready to make some big changes.

I have enjoyed unwavering support from my husband, family and friends and previous work colleagues. Balancing motherhood, family and career adds a different dimension to my life experience, which I bring to coaching. However, I have also found specific knowledge and experience is not a prerequisite to successful client outcomes. Coaching works on a 'stand-alone' basis. The coach is not 'the expert', but a facilitator for unlocking the client's full potential through the coaching process.

Any personal sacrifices along the way have been 'having' sacrifices and I can honestly say that I have not missed them at all. For me, the extensive benefits have far outweighed the costs. I feel a satisfaction in achievement that I have never felt before in my life. I enjoy and savour the here and now, and can positively visualise my future, knowing I have regained control of my life. **99**

As mentioned above, one essential element of living your best life is 'living for today'. We all waste far too much of our precious time thinking about 'life after when' and what things will be like on that fictitious day when we have absolutely everything we want. However, as that famous saying goes, a successful life is all about enjoying the journey, not the destination.

## Life is not a dress rehearsal

**VANESSA WESTWELL**

❝ How often do you take the time to make space for a fun activity in your busy schedule? Do you avoid taking lunch with a friend or colleague because you are 'too busy?' Yet how productive are you when you grab a sandwich at your desk?

A lot of life is about making the best of what we've got – whether it is getting the most done in the time we spend at our office, having the most useful discussions at a meeting, or really listening to a loved one when they tell us about their day.

Contrary to popular belief, life is about quality not quantity!

I remember a conversation I had with a friend in her early thirties who vowed she would rather die than live to be old and infirm. 'I want to be shot when I get too old', she proclaimed, with all the arrogance of her 'youth'. She would rather be dead than live a restricted life, with no friends and family to support or love her. Quality of life was the key for her.

Yet my elderly neighbour, a still young-at-heart 90-year-old, gives thanks out loud for every new morning. He feels blessed that he is alive to appreciate the sunshine, the birds, his friendly neighbours, and any other small facet of his world. He is living a quality life suitable for someone of his age, and still looks forward to activities with hope in his heart and a smile on his face.

I find his optimism infectious. I want to be that way when I get old. But I also want to be that way today.

One way to wring the most out of life is to 'live in the moment'. Use all your senses to feel what you feel when you feel it, to be wholly in your life, as it happens, here and now. Rather than thinking about what you haven't achieved, write down all the things you have got now. Rather than worry about the future or regret the past, enjoy the moment now.

Life is not a dress rehearsal for something else. Get out there and play your part today! ❞

# 8 Problems, progress and diversity

> Life is like a game of cards. The hand that is dealt you is determinism; the way you play it is free will.
>
> NEHRU

TRAINING TO be a coach is a journey. Like many great journeys, people set out with the best of intentions. They know where they're headed, are firmly committed and clear about where they're going, know what the finishing point will look like and what their reward will be. Trouble is, life being life invariably throws a spanner or two in the works and all sorts of things can happen along the way to impede progress.

At the end of the residential weekend when trainees are given details of their coursework, they are also asked to submit a learning plan estimating how long they think it will take them to complete the course. Much scratching of heads often results. How long? 'As long as it takes', seems the only sensible answer – what's the point in committing to anything else? The point, as Pam, the Head of Distance Learning, and the other support staff know, is that without a plan, nothing gets done. 'Failing to plan is planning to fail' as someone once said.

The work that you need to do in order to complete the course isn't something you can fit in during the commercial breaks in between your favourite TV programmes. A real commitment of time and organisation is needed if you're going to do it, which is why you're asked for a plan. Support can then be offered if and when it becomes clear that – for whatever reason – you are starting to fall badly behind.

Illness, family problems, pressure of work, can all slow you down – plus, family, friends or colleagues can start to feel threatened and start to sabotage things when it becomes clear that you aren't going to be the comfortable 'old self' that you were, ever again. So over the weeks, support can start to ebb away leaving the trainee wondering if they have made the right decision and whether the aggravation is worth it.

# Before coaching I wouldn't have been able to cope

SHEREE RACKHAM

**66** If it wasn't for my life coaching course and appreciating what coaching has done for me as both an individual and a coach I hate to think where I'd be. From having what I thought was a great life, it all went belly up last October. After that, if it hadn't been for life coaching I could have suffered some sort of nervous breakdown.

I believe that all through life things are thrown at us, some good, some bad, some gruelling and some sad, but I would probably say that from October last year, I have had one of the most challenging times in my life. Whereas before the coaching I wouldn't have been able to cope, I have coped and come through it. Yes I still get stressed and I reckon I have increased my number of grey hairs tenfold, but I actually take a step back now and think of how to deal with a situation and then don't get so stressed.

I don't rush into things and if I have a crisis I deal with it. My blood pressure is so much better, I'm happier, healthier and I am enjoying life much more than I thought I could. And things get done and problems get solved sooner rather than later. It's rubbed off on people around me, I'm better to be around, and as I know that life coaching works, I can use my skills to help others. **99**

In completing the coach training course work, anecdotal evidence indicates that those who are used to studying find it easier to complete the reading and the written work, though this is not necessarily always the case. The written work is, after all, not a thesis or a technical handbook but requires the student to give a great deal of themselves and is judged more on content than such things as grammar or spelling.

On the other hand, those who may be good academically often struggle with the practice element; they feel uncomfortable and exposed in a coaching conversation. Even those who in their own words can 'talk the hind legs off a donkey' don't necessarily find the practice work easy for, of course, coaching isn't about talking – it's about listening.

What all this means is that trainees need support right throughout their coaching journey, and as you will have read in the Introduction, this is one of the most vital elements around which Rivas Palmer's approach has been built. No one's going to bother you if you're pressing on and making good progress, but if you need a friendly voice and someone to help remind you of the answer to 'Why on earth did I think I could do this?' then there's always someone at hand.

Here, Geraldine Thalmessinger, Head of Membership at Rivas Palmer, explains her role as on-line agony aunt and sounding board, and the reward she gets from being able to guide students through to the achievement of their goal:

## People are enormously grateful ... I am incredibly energised

**GERALDINE THALMESSINGER**

❝ My role is to support Rivas Palmer students in any way I can. Often they ring in for advice and in effect, I end up giving them a mini coaching session in which I ask them what they think they can do to overcome their difficulties or obstacles.

The types of worries and problems they have vary enormously and often reflect why they came to take up coach training in the first place, for example:

- Many aren't happy in their current job – it may be too stressful, depressing or they have simply lost enthusiasm for it. This can create lethargy and a general feeling of hopelessness.
- Some are really desperate to get out of their job and want to throw it all in immediately and they are frustrated at having to wait.
- Some want to embark upon this new adventure straight away and don't want to be bothered with the training – they tend not to put the effort into learning thoroughly and effectively sabotage themselves and slow things up.
- Some have been made redundant and have either spent their redundancy settlement or can see it trickling away and are fearful that the training won't put them in a better position.
- Many have financial worries and wonder if they should get a job or persevere with coach training in the hope that it will bring them an income at the end

Often when people are fearful, I advise them to read Susan Jeffers' book *'Feel the fear and do it anyway'* – an excellent guide to achieving more than you could ever imagine simply through grasping the nettle and taking the first step. Certainly it's a highly motivational text and often really helps in getting people going again.

Unfortunately there are also those who have fallen ill or are having to nurse or support a family member, and they contact me to tell me that they will have to withdraw. I invariably tell them to keep in touch and not give up, and of course that we will welcome them back whenever they are in a position to resume their training.

We're certainly not an organisation that says 'Do it our way, in line with our timescales, or you're out'. Our whole focus is on doing everything possible to ensure our students succeed and that at the end of the course they're confident and highly competent coaches who stay part of our family. Even more than that, we want our students to get what they want to out of the course – it's all about them ultimately, not about us.

People react and perform in different ways to the challenge of coach training: some are low in confidence and self-esteem and fear they will be unable to do the course work. Others are highly excited by the course work and extremely keen – for example one student went straight home from the residential weekend and wrote 500 words of his assignment that very night!

Generally though, about two thirds need to find confidence and the belief that they can not only do the course work, but can become great coaches. Those who don't have a job can be particularly low in self-esteem and it's my role to help them see the value they can bring to the rest of the world through skills and traits that they consider worthless.

I contact people initially a few days after they have completed the residential weekend to tell them that I offer support, inviting them to call me if they want to. But after that I give them the choice of whether or not they want to keep in touch. At present I speak to about 40 people a week. I find they are enormously grateful and would do anything not to let me down; such is the bond of the relationship we build.

For my part, doing this job just keeps me incredibly energized, although you'd assume it would be really tiring. I just love people, which gives me motivation – and I guess it's this that keeps my energy going. I listen to them, give them focus, praise them and boost their self-esteem. It's not hard and it's certainly not false; their faith in me and Rivas Palmer is what gives me faith in them. For example, one student told me they'd done a piece of their written work but lacked the confidence to send it in – how rewarding it was for me to be able to help them conquer that fear of rejection! I really do believe at times that I get more out of it than the students.

People contact me for a huge variety of reasons, but some of the most common are:

- Because they have made mistakes in learning, or are struggling with the work.
- To ask for constructive feedback on what they are thinking and doing.
- To seek direction on how they should tackle the work, what they should do next.

I always try to be non-judgmental and empathetic; after all we all suffer problems of some sort and can all benefit from encouragement and praise along the way. **99**

Whether or not trainees take advantage of Geraldine's support, each is assigned a mentor coach whose purpose is to help their students get to grips with the finer points of the practical coaching requirements and also to help generally by answering queries and providing encouragement. There's just no way a trainee can slip through the net!

## The more you listen to people the more they tune in to you

TIM WATTS

**66** The best aspects of the training have been sharing with other people, particularly in respect of the practical side of the training. Rivas Palmer is a FAMILY and is very good at this.

The main challenges have been finding time to do the work while working and having a family life (I have three teenage sons). I am comfortable with the written requirement having had to do this at university and at work. The biggest challenge has been becoming comfortable with listening to people on the telephone while coaching and being entirely focused on them. For me to say nothing while they talk and think is difficult. Yet the more you listen to people the more they tune into you and you get everything by doing nothing.

I'm a fervent supporter of Rivas Palmer's support network. Geraldine, my mentor, has been fantastic with helping me move forward. **99**

Another channel providing on-going support to trainee coaches and qualified coaches alike is the national network of coaching circles. The advantage of these is that they are held on a local or regional basis, usually monthly, and are a forum where coaches can share ideas and market knowledge, collaborate... or simply have a glass of wine and a chat. They certainly provide evidence of the caring, sharing nature of the majority of coaches and can be a great source of inspiration and support for those coaches who work alone and know they need to get out more!

> Life's most persistent and urgent question is 'What are you doing for others?'
>
> **MARTIN LUTHER KING JNR**

## I have found what I was searching for and am enjoying my career once again

**SHAUN TODD**

❝ Being an HR and Development professional for 15 years specialising in diversity and work-life balance, becoming a consultant and having my work published meant I had achieved all my goals. Now I was looking for something new that used my skills, experience and 'credibility'. I was tired of corporate politics and wanted to work with people on a one-to-one basis. People who actively sought change, not how best to avoid it!

Turning an interest (and qualifications) in complimentary therapy into a new career was one possible avenue, but this did not meet my need to help people realise their full potential and make use of my extensive HR and Development skills.

I wanted to move forward, not backward, while still achieving work-life balance, with flexible and part-time working hours that would allow me to work from home.

Only when I saw the Rivas Palmer advert did it all click into place – a professional career that would build on my skills and experience, allow me to work with individuals and help them develop holistically. There was even the benefit of achieving my 'impossible' goal of owning a dog while working.

Before, during and after qualifying as an accredited life coach I knew I had found what I was searching for and was enjoying a career once again.

Family, friends and colleagues commented that my 'sparkle' had returned, and I knew even before my clients and their positive testimonials started to arrive that I had found my new 'improved' profession. And yes, the puppy arrived shortly afterwards …

I really enjoy working with my clients. They are busy professionals who realise business and personal performance are linked to success in other areas of life, for example, family, health and leisure. Often however, development activities focus only on 'business', and do not explore those areas outside work that can be the key to further success (or failure).

I help them find their own answers by providing objectivity; time and space to think and plan; a confidential sounding board to explore new ideas; techniques and support to gain new understanding, and alternative approaches for action leading to success.

Continuous professional development is important so I actively support the profession by running the Oxford Coaching Circle where I have regular meetings with my coaching friends and colleagues.

I am also launching my own product range for caring professional coaches and their clients which I think is important, as there does not seem to be anything specifically for us. **"**

As well as a commitment to providing ongoing, proactive support, another of Rivas Palmer's great concerns is to raise the standing of coaching and to ensure that all their coaches work to the highest possible levels of integrity, honesty and quality. In line with this it has developed its own Code of Conduct that all trainers, mentor coaches and students are required to abide by. Although coaches start to use this when training, many also adopt it as their own Code of Conduct after accreditation.

## The Rivas Palmer Code of Conduct

- All coaches must conduct themselves with dignity, honesty, integrity and responsibility.
- Clients must be assured that anything they discuss in a coaching session must remain confidential unless required by law, or the client gives permission in writing.
- Coaches must not be judgmental or give unwelcome advice.

- Coaches must be clear about the boundary between coaching and other therapies, such as counselling.
- Coaches must not recommend a specific therapist unless qualified to do so.
- Coaches must not bring Rivas Palmer into disrepute in any way.
- Coaches must not give misleading information about coaching and its benefits.
- Coaches must not make claims about the outcome of coaching unless able to provide evidence.
- All coaching agreements must be easy to understand, with expectations of both the coach and the client clearly stated.
- Coaches must not coach minors (under 18s) without parents' written permission.
- Coaches must be willing to recommend other coaches if it is more appropriate for the client.
- Coaches must be willing to share skills and information with other members of Rivas Palmer.
- Coaches must take out professional indemnity insurance.
- Whenever possible, coaches are encouraged to raise the profile of coaching and correct any misconceptions about what coaching is and isn't.
- Coaches must treat all clients in a way that is respectful of people's differences in relating to disability, gender, age, race, religion and sexual orientation.

The advantage for students of this Code of Conduct is that it gives them guidelines for the way they should conduct themselves in a coaching situation, and a stable framework within which to work. This can be invaluable, particularly at the start of their coaching careers when they are struggling with putting a whole new skill set into practice.

## I'm on a high one minute and in the pits, the next

MAXINE PEACHEY | 66 Coaching has hit me like a brick. Before I started, I knew about it through work (I work in training) and through my membership of the CIPD (Chartered Institute of Personnel and Development), but even so, I didn't know much about the impact it could have. I guess I just thought it was talking to people – not much more than that.

My employers have supported me with taking this course and it was only ever my intention to use it to broaden my skills base for work. It certainly has helped with that, particularly in areas like the values and skills workshops I now run. However, as I'm now getting closer to accreditation, I know that I want to use coaching in different ways, and I'm currently negotiating to start working part-time so I can develop my own coaching practice.

I actually came across the Rivas Palmer course on the internet, and something about it just drew me to it. I know someone else at work who has done the course and she had researched other courses more than I had. Her comments reinforced the benefits of Rivas Palmer's approach and some of the drawbacks of other courses in terms of their fee structure and lack of ongoing support.

With coaching I've found I'm on a high one minute and in the pits the next. I think that's all to do with the way it makes you look at yourself, the way it makes you open up. I've seen evidence of that around me too; since I've become involved with coaching, I've noticed people actively *want* to be around me. Something about me now must be drawing people to me.

I now realise that for most of us, our self-awareness is completely untapped, we just exist on a very superficial level. Self-awareness and self-development are paramount and I believe that as a coach you need to understand yourself before you can help others.

Coaching changes the way you speak to people and the way you understand them. It makes you both more tolerant and more intolerant. For example, I really listen to the children now, really sit down and listen to what they're saying, not just make assumptions about what I think they need or want, or what their views are. But on the other hand I'm now more intolerant of other people's lack of effort. I know that through coaching they could have so much more.

Although most people are interested in what I'm doing, not everyone is supportive. For instance a friend recently said, 'How can you be a coach when your own life isn't sorted out?' Fortunately, I can live with comments like this. I think, actually, that a lot of it is down to fear, and a feeling that perhaps there is a better way and they are missing out.

Certainly I have valued the support of Rivas Palmer at every level. You can phone and talk to a real person and they actually care about you and your viewpoint and your problems. If I'd had to rely just on the support of my friends as I undertook the course, I know I would have dropped out by now; they just don't understand enough about what I'm doing and what coaching is about.

Rivas Palmer's staff don't push, but they motivate. I find writing difficult and not particularly enjoyable, so the written work has been a bit of a challenge. With all the reading and all the new concepts there just seems so much information to absorb, and trying to filter and sort through it and put my thoughts into words has been quite a challenge.

I guess I still have a 'school' mentality, looking to write pieces that the teacher will approve of, rather than – as I know is right – putting down my own thoughts and using the exercise in the way it's intended, that is, as a means for helping me learn and summarise my learning experience. Recently I went on holiday with one of my study buddies from the course. We had intended to make it a working holiday – working at our coaching written work – and as luck would have it, the weather wasn't very good so we were able to do quite a bit and really help each other along.

For me, coaching is and has been a very positive experience, although I've never been through so many highs and lows. I'm hoping now I'm nearing accreditation and my coaching skills and confidence are growing, that things will move forward on a more even keel.

For anyone thinking of going into coaching, I would recommend the Rivas Palmer course to anyone, absolutely and unconditionally. **99**

One of the questions that often emerges when people are enquiring about a career in coaching, or even just asking about coaching in general terms, is 'What's the difference between male and female coaches?' You can see why they'd ask. Not only does coaching often deal with very intimate, personal issues (the sort of thing that some people think some men might shy away from), but it does seem to be a profession which is largely colonized by women.

# If it ain't broke, don't fix it!

BELINDA MOLLROSS

66 Are there any differences between men and women in coaching? The main differences I've observed is that some men will tend to naturally like or be drawn to particular issues, and there will be others that they will think are frippery, and won't really consider seriously. But in coaching the fact that the client or student has come up with that issue means that it means something to them. Therefore, you have to put aside your judgement.

I think some men find it difficult to do that. I wouldn't say all men, at all. For example, I have seen a male student coach another female student whose goal was a bit, shall we say, insubstantial and 'girly'. But he was completely and utterly brilliant; whatever he really thought of the subject was never evident throughout the session. He did a spectacular job, and he will be a spectacular coach.

But I've seen other students, male students predominantly, who've had an issue with getting out of the 'fix it' mentality, as that's been the approach they've been used to taking. Those who have already got to the stage of accreditation find it's no longer an issue; but those who haven't dealt with that side of their masculinity have to go through that struggle before they can get there.

Some of them, whether consciously or unconsciously, feel that they don't want to get into difficulties with dealing with some of the topics which might emerge in personal coaching, so they plan to go into business, executive or corporate coaching, hoping that this will keep them away from 'personal' topics. They could be in for a shock!

You wonder what the attraction of coaching is to them really. Certainly it's a false logic, as even in business coaching anything can come up. I've had business executives crying – even though I've never suggested we talk about anything that was personal.

But it's not a foregone conclusion that coaching will always come round to personal issues. It doesn't if you've got a business person who is clearly focused on business or project issues. If they stay focused, then the personal bit may not come into it at all. But with others it does – perhaps their attitude at work is coming out of something that's going on at home, or vice versa, and then you get the overlap. 99

Belinda's view is based on many years of coaching and mentoring student coaches. But what do others think? As I wrote this book I asked many people what, if anything, they thought were the differences between men and women in coaching and there was remarkable consensus in their answers:

- Generally there are no particular differences which can be related purely to gender.
- Both men and women can make equally excellent coaches.
- If there are any differences it is that women sometimes struggle more than men with lack of confidence when starting to coach, whereas men have to try harder initially to be totally objective and not offer advice in the coaching relationship.

GARY LAFFERTY | 66 Although I think both men and women make equally good coaches, I think that women sometimes are more successful at running coaching businesses than men because they consciously or subconsciously take on the challenge of pushing themselves to be successful. They concentrate this into feelings of having to do things better or certainly the best they can, in order to justify and reinforce their self-belief. 99

So, no discrimination, no 'innate ability', no excuses – great coaches are those of either sex who work hard, are fascinated by people, really listen to what others have to say, and want always to keep learning.

## Effective coaches can come from anywhere

TIM WATTS | 66 I believe that effective coaches can come from anywhere and have any sort of a background, though I would be surprised if anyone younger than 25 was really good – I don't believe they would have enough life experience.

I find it interesting to see so many women active in coaching having come from a world where men are more prevalent. I believe, rightly or wrongly, that industry is more attuned to the natural resources of men; so being a man stands me in good stead for coaching in the corporate world. However, men typically aren't sensitive enough to make really good coaches so I can see why many people are drawn to working with women in life coaching. Certainly the training has blessed me with more sensitivity and emotional intelligence than previously.

> There is a tendency for some individuals to become so fascinated with how they might change that they never get round to actually doing anything.
>
> NICHOLAS BATE, BEING THE BEST

# 9 Coaching, or playing shop?

> You can't build a reputation on what you're going to do.
> **HENRY FORD**

BY NO means everyone undertakes coach training with a view to setting up in business as a coach, but for those who do, there's one point they can't afford to ignore. Starting up as a coach is no different to setting up any other kind of business. If you don't focus on the business and keep that focus, you will never be successful – it's not enough just to be a good coach.

Government statistics show that there has been a recent dramatic increase in the numbers of people setting up businesses in the area of 'personal support' such as counselling, fitness training, aromatherapy, and of course, coaching. Whilst this makes some aspiring coaches feel nervous about the competition, it is usually the case in business that competition is a good thing and proves that a market exists to sustain these types of businesses.

However, what it also means is that as competition becomes more fierce, the good will prosper and grow and those who aren't will suffer and eventually go under. That's true of any type of business, not just coaching. Statistics show that a disturbingly high number of small businesses fail within the first year, many more within the first three years. The problem isn't usually lack of a good service or product offering, but 'business' related issues such as cash flow and marketing.

What then is the secret of success for those who do set up and maintain successful coaching practices? The answer is – exactly the same things that lead to success in any other business:

1 High levels of motivation
2 Sound management
3 Effective and ongoing marketing

Gary Lafferty is Rivas Palmer's 'Mr Marketing' and here he explains his role and outlines what he believes are the essential ingredients for success in running a coaching business:

## Finding and promoting what's right for you

GARY LAFFERTY

❝ I think Rivas Palmer are incredibly supportive of their students and I am proud to be part of their team. I first got to know Natasha about four years ago when I was a member of the British Business Advisors and Trainers Academy, and since then our parallel paths have increasingly converged.

I became part of the team when they set up the company and since then have worked with them delivering marketing training as part of the residential weekend, through a specific marketing training module, and through teleclasses and mentoring and support.

Although I am not a coach myself, I am a passionate supporter of coaching and a lot of what I do and have always done in advising my business clients is now known as 'coaching'. I believe that Rivas Palmer are unique in the emphasis they place on giving their students the practical knowledge and support they need to set up a coaching business – if that's what they want to do – and also providing ongoing support as their businesses grow.

Setting up a coaching business is no different to setting up any other kind of business. You need to develop business skills and acumen; keep an eye on practicalities such as cash flow and tax, and demonstrate self-discipline and stamina – plus perseverance when things aren't as easy as you'd hoped. None of these is easier for coaches than anyone else, perhaps harder in some ways because some coaches have never previously had much exposure to business life and the accompanying challenges.

That said, I don't think any one type or category of person or any particular background makes a more successful coach than any other. The most successful are those with determination, enthusiasm and the motivation to just keep going and keep trying new things until they find the formula that works for them. That's the same whether your background was as a housewife or a successful business executive.

I believe that to be successful, coaches need to concentrate less on hiding behind the label of 'coach' and more on the results that they can produce using coaching as a tool. In coaching, as any other type of business, it's important to be clear about your unique selling points and the niche market to which you want to appeal. If you simply say 'I'm a coach, come and get me', you won't succeed. That's also an important point in terms of differentiating yourself from the amount of competition about. If you're a generalist, there will appear to be lots of other people doing the same thing – so how is a prospective client going to identify and choose you?

However, if you specialise, the client can immediately identify whether or not he or she needs your specific services and you make yourself unique because there is only you doing exactly what it is that you do to produce unique benefits for your particular clients.

Marketing a coaching practice is just like marketing any other type of business. Whatever the business, there is one crucial key to success and that's self-belief, both belief in what you are offering and also belief that you can market. Both are absolutely vital, and that's why many successful business people and coaches have their own coaches. They have a coach to help them generate and maintain this strong belief in themselves.

Any type of person can be good at business, there's not one standard personality type, or recommended approach that works better than any other. You can be equally effective taking a quiet, measured focused approach as someone who is louder, more extravert and dramatic; it's just finding and promoting what's right for you and not pretending to be someone or something you're not.

In addition to self-belief, there are three key steps to follow:

1  Set your goal

2  Formulate a plan

3  Write a 'to do' list

It sounds easy and it is! The hard part, the bit that people struggle with the most – either as coaches or in any other type of business – is marketing and keeping at it continuously; not thinking 'I've got some clients now, so I can stop.' People literally seem to forget that they need to keep filling the sales pipeline at the top so that they're continuously replenishing the pool of people who may be interested in their services.

Oddly enough, although all of this should fit in really well with the essence of coaching – the goal setting, motivation, reviewing options and action; in fact, it's often the case of the cobbler's children… Coaches tend not to remember to apply all this to themselves and what they're doing, which again is why coaches often need coaches to help them succeed and keep going.

Anyone can be good at marketing and run a successful business – it's definitely an area where I'm totally non-judgmental about who might fail and who might succeed. Yes, it can be difficult if you're very shy simply because you need to approach people and let them know about your services. Even so, I have known plenty of people who have considered themselves shy who have gone on to achieve incredible success simply because their passion and enthusiasm helped them overcome their natural inclination to hold back.

It's also absolutely the case that people seem to blossom and make a real breakthrough when they first have some success through their marketing. The energy surge they get when it all suddenly starts to come together is fantastic – I get lots of feedback from students or qualified coaches saying 'I did so and so and it worked – just like you said it would. Now I'm flying!'

People find marketing daunting, but it isn't as long as you follow the process:

- Learn everything you can about marketing – through books, tapes, articles, seminars, or whatever.
- Have your own coach to support you in developing your marketing.
- Make marketing a priority in your life on a daily and weekly basis.
- Have fun – like anything else, if you don't enjoy it, why would anyone else find it attractive?

In any business, it's important to keep asking yourself and your clients, 'What else can I do?' 'How can I do more?' 'What can I do better?' By constantly stretching yourself in this way, you are ensuring that you continuously improve and grow in what you're doing. But, of course, doing this takes time – you have to consciously set aside time to spend on yourself and on developing your business. Don't just bang on doing the same things in the same way over and over again – that's really not the most productive way for you to help other people.

### There is the potential for success in everyone

I absolutely love training coaching students. I get a lot of enjoyment and energy from the room and this is reflected in my own high energy levels when working with the groups – they give me an enormous buzz.

What drives me and keeps me focused is my belief that there is the potential for success in everyone. If I can help people release that success and realize their goals then I feel that's what I'm here to do. I really believe what I say when I tell them 'your success is my success'. I also believe they're all going to do well, which is why I leave each training session feeling so energized and uplifted. And the best compliment I ever get is when someone contacts me to say, 'Gary, I tried what you said and it really worked for me.'

I think coaching is a truly commendable activity and it fits with the way that society and business is currently evolving. In the next five years I believe that we might see coaching re-packaged and called something else, but it will still essentially be coaching and there will still be a need, in fact an even greater need, for great coaches.

In my view, a lot of what coaching comes down to is that 'the answers are inside us'; and regardless of what the questions and issues are, coaches can help us set those answers free, and help us develop in the ways we need to and want to. With increasing use of coaching, the world will definitely become a better place.

If someone told me today that they thought they wanted to become a coach and asked me whether I thought it was a good idea, I guess I'd advise them to consider it carefully. For one thing, I believe that whatever you're thinking of doing that's new, you should never jump, but always step. Also, I believe that although everyone can benefit from coaching, not everyone can necessarily be a good coach. I would define 'a good coach' as someone who has a genuine desire for someone else's well being; everything else tends to follow on from that. You need good self-belief and certainly, belief in others; those are the two crucial characteristics.

Once someone has reached the stage of being a good coach however, I believe that everyone has the potential within them to market themselves successfully and have a fantastic and profitable business. **99**

Gary's training in marketing and sales is effective, motivating and highly energising, providing that essential 'missing link' between having coaching skills and being able to practise effectively and profitably as a coach.

## It works!

EMMA FAIRCHILD | 66 Here I am, just over three weeks since receiving accreditation and I am jumping with excitement! I now have eight paying clients and more referrals coming in from my clients and practice clients! What can I say about the Rivas Palmer marketing course? IT WORKS!! 99

JOHN BLAKEY | 66 Our company, *121 coaching* has successfully implemented a number of the marketing techniques learnt directly from the Rivas Palmer course. These range from the production of business cards, web sites and brochures to the forming of partnerships and the use of the 'five-step' closing approach to convert interested prospects into real, paying clients. We are convinced this part of the course has accelerated the development of our business. 99

As mentioned in Chapter 6, one of the foundation stones of the coaching process is that the coach has to learn that the coaching relationship 'isn't about you, it's about them'. This can also be a highly useful and profitable approach to carry forward into the business arena.

## Being aware of and sensitive to others

LESLEY BUCKERIDGE | 66 After listening to Gary I included a goal about having 'referral only' clients to my business plan along with a paragraph about 'extreme care'. I had unconsciously been using this technique since we started the company – following up regularly, sending personal notes, small gifts, cards, etc. I didn't realise other people did this. I didn't appreciate how powerful this activity was and how much impact it has had on our success. But when Gary talked about it he made me realize it was a well-recognised technique and marketing tool. Doh!

As a stakeholder in the business, it is in my interest to encourage the team to adopt this policy as it will make us more successful and more profitable.

Also, at a recent meeting I consciously matched my energy levels to those of a prospective client and was able to develop a good rapport. Normally I am like Tigger from Winnie the Pooh, irrespective of how others are being. Whilst I'll never want to change (happy in my skin), being aware and sensitive to others and adapting a bit to reflect their preferred communication style and energy levels, at least until rapport is established, won't kill me!

The trick is to be aware of what is happening i.e. the difference between 'doing' and 'being'. 'Doing' is easy. 'Being' is a toughy, but I'm working on it. **

There is no doubt that for everyone it takes time to establish a successful business and one of the key factors for success is to progress gradually and steadily ('step, don't jump'). But this can be hard for newly qualified coaches who are thrilled by coaching. They just want to get on and DO it! However, without a business plan, business experience (or advice from those

> Don't go round saying the world owes you a living. The world owes you nothing; it was here first. **MARK TWAIN**

who have it) and the ability to balance their enthusiasm with relentless hard work and perseverance, often over long periods of time, establishing a coaching business can be almost impossible.

## I couldn't wait to become my own boss

SUE CLARK

** My message is that sticking with the day job is important. Without wishing to be negative, I learnt the hard way and I don't want anyone else suffering like I have.

I went from full-time to part-time work around the time I qualified as a coach last year and I couldn't wait to become a full-time coach, to be my own boss and work at something I truly enjoyed. But I got carried away with my ideas and, not satisfied with making do and working from home in my spare time, I took out a bank loan so I could pay the deposit and rent on an office that was 'mine'.

At the same time I became more and more discontented with working part-time in a job that paid £5 an hour when I knew I was worth so much more so I quit my job to concentrate on my business.

But the reality was that the business didn't come in all that quick, and there I was stuck with bills, a loan to repay and hardly any money coming in. I hopped from office to therapy centre thinking what a great business opportunity it would be and let myself be led into thinking that by reinvesting my office deposit into renting a therapy room, business would boom. The truth was I had *no* business whatsoever at the therapy centre and felt terribly let down.

The consequences were almost disastrous. I used our savings to help keep paying for my business overheads, and it is not a nice feeling to use your own money to keep paying for bills which really should never have been there.

Now I am in a position where I am struggling to keep my business account topped up, and I am having to find a full-time job. I have come full circle it seems and I am finding it hard not to be downhearted about the whole experience. My husband has supported me fully in what he thought were good business ideas, except they weren't. I have learnt some lessons.

But don't get me wrong, being coached and becoming a coach is the best thing I ever did and I still benefit from having a coach of my own so I still believe in it completely.

And my story is not meant to say, 'this will happen to you'. Plenty of people take risks and live through them with a smile. But my three biggest tips are:

1   Don't give up the day job until you have enough business to keep you afloat for six months.

2   Get as much practice as you can before and after you have qualified – the more clients you have, the more referrals you may get.

3   Keep being coached yourself, even if it is just by one of your study buddies. Support is so important and I can think of no better way than coaching to help you through difficult times.

I've learnt some lessons now and at least I am able to celebrate the fact I have survived my first year. **99**

So, the message is take it slowly, and don't be seduced by the siren song of an expensive office, ritzy IT equipment, a fancy car, expensive brochure, or any of the other 'love to have' tangible elements of running a business. None of it is necessary for business success. Distilled to a very basic level, what you need to concentrate on is the 'being' and 'doing' aspects of being in business; the 'having' will then soon follow.

## The loneliness of the long-distance coach

Another important thing that people sometimes overlook when they contemplate working for themselves – coaching or doing anything else – is how lonely it can be. Carrying sole responsibility for doing everything can be a great burden.

So, you need to consider at the outset whether you have the physical and mental strength, determination, tenacity, self-discipline and self-belief to run a business and where – if anywhere – you will find the encouragement and support to keep you going when things get tough. Friends and family may be kind and concerned, but often their interest in your business and understanding of what you're facing just aren't enough.

## Life can move on and leave you behind

BELINDA MOLLROSS

66 Working for yourself is a lot different to working for a company and because of this, there are many good ideas for new businesses that never get off the drawing board. For a start, you have to know whether or not you're suited to working on your own, and a lot of people aren't.

This can be for three reasons:

1  They're rubbish at time management.

2  They have difficulty putting a price on their services because they've always been used to someone else dictating what they're worth.

3  They are social people and when they're no longer going out to work, they can't stand the isolation. So, you find that most coaches do a variety of work, because you have to have that social contact.

Also, if you're solely at home you tend to lose your connection to what is happening in the world. For example, when you're employed, you're aware of what's going on in the office because you gossip and talk about what problems people are having; there's far more day-to-day interaction. So the further you are from having that daily influence, the easier it is for your ideas to become outdated and you find yourself stuck in a time warp.

The classic scenario is immigrants – when people emigrate to another country they take their culture with them and it stays at that point, so they bring their children up in that same culture. Then the kids go and visit the relatives 'back home' and discover everybody there has moved on. They don't do those sorts of things any more! So, if as a coach you become too isolated you can be stuck in a time warp about what the current issues are that people are having problems with. Even simple things like, whether the travel is as bad as it was when you were going to work.

Yes, I think that phrase 'You need to get out more' can be very true! **99**

> You are in control of your destiny and success. The universe will take care of some things for you but not everything. You have to play your part too. **GARY LAFFERTY**

Earlier in this chapter, we looked at the key elements for success in running any business. These are vital, but there are also a number of 'essentials' that pertain specifically to running a coaching practice. These have been distilled from interviews with many people I spoke to in compiling this book. In their view, if you want to develop a successful coaching practice, the following elements are both necessary and desirable:

- Maintaining and developing true passion for the process, truly 'walking the talk'.
- Committing to life-long learning and being 'the best one can be'.
- Harnessing that enthusiasm into a step-by-step business vision and marketing plan.
- Creating a practice that is unique and founded on your own core skills and personality.
- Continuously marketing and networking.

None of that sounds difficult. But then, nothing about running a business is ever difficult on paper!

## The more I find out, the more I discover there is so much more to know

JULIA MILES | **66** Way back in 2002 I was asked to attend a discussion on a local radio station – I duly arrived at the station and was asked to wait. Sitting in the room was a lady and I walked over and introduced myself. Later during our conversation I found out that she was (and still is) a life coach.

I asked her what life coaching was, she explained – and

................eureka

..............this was it

..........wow

........this is what it had all been about

...this was where I wanted, no *needed*, to be.

This, I knew, tied together all the strands of everything that had happened before in my life – it felt as though a glorious tapestry could now be woven.

I rushed home and went on the internet to find all I could about coaching only to find a myriad of coach training opportunities out there. Which was the one for me? I contacted Sarah – the lady whom I had spoken to – for her advice and she sent me the literature from Rivas Palmer. I read through it and it sounded… what did it sound like? Well, very honest, and exciting and true and right. I went along to a presentation and met Natasha and the team and just KNEW this was right. I knew I had found IT.

I signed up for the course in February 2003. Going to the course I felt a mixture of excitement and trepidation. On arrival, I was met by the team and I immediately felt at home. This feeling of being 'at home' and 'one of a family' has never left me since.

The course was amazing …

– it opened my eyes to things I had never realised and to things I thought I knew.

– it opened my mind to all the tremendous possibilities that I had and the world had.

– it opened my heart to everything – the great potential and just everything.

To say that my life has not been the same since might seem too dramatic, but it's true – I see so much more, I feel so much more, and I know so much more. This is a lifestyle – it is not just a job, a training course, a book with words in. The more I discover, the more I know there is more to discover and the deeper I go the more I find depth.

Following the course I left my full time job and started on the scary but exhilarating journey of self-employment. Rivas Palmer very wisely gives a workshop on marketing your business and I use this knowledge to the full now.

I quickly realised that starting your own business did not happen overnight (the magic fairy with the wand was not real!). Then I thought – 'if you planted a seed in your garden you would not expect to go out the next morning and see a flower – instead you would nurture that seed and water it and tend it and then one day you would see the flower'. This is how to look upon your new business.

I decided (using my new skills of goal setting) that I would initially build on what I had been doing for more than eight years so that I still had an income. I had been an outplacement consultant (a bit like recruitment in reverse!) so I networked and ended up with some work within that sphere.

The coach in me really started to have an effect there and I've been very successful with that work – gaining several large contracts with top companies. Through my new coaching skills I expanded on how I work with clients and because I'm a coach I know what questions to ask to really get them thinking. My contracts keep coming and from this I have picked up some private outplacement work too. Once that was sorted and I knew the bills were being paid I concentrated on refining, expanding my coaching.

Throughout all this, the team at Rivas Palmer have been there with me every step of the way, encouraging me through emails and phone calls, inviting me to get-togethers and always keeping me fully informed about what's going on in the coaching world.

I've coached individuals on a wide range of issues and found a real 'buzz' from knowing that I'm making a difference. I decided to journey further down the path of coaching and have attended some more courses since then and have discovered what I always suspected – the more I find out the more I know there is so much more to know. This coaching journey is infinite

I cannot believe the difference this has made to my life – all of my life – not just the professional aspect. I feel that my future in coaching is not going to work out how I thought initially, but it's actually bigger, wider, deeper, more meaningful.

I have several plans now as to how I can use the knowledge that I have accumulated to make a difference and the feeling that gives me is one, I think, akin to floating in a huge vat of chocolate!!!!!!!!!!!!!!!

Since I've become a coach I keep 'words of wisdom' when I hear them and read them and one that I'd like to share now is –

*'Don't ask yourself what the world needs*

*ask yourself what makes you come alive*

*and then go do it*

*because what the world needs is people who have come alive.'*

Thank you to Rivas Palmer for showing me how to come alive. **99**

Even for those with business experience, running a coaching practice is never easy, simply because you are required to do many things you have never done before, some of which you feel you are not terribly good at. It's all part of running a small business and having to do everything yourself. On the other hand, when you are successful you can bask in the full glory of what you – and only you – have been able to achieve.

## You have to leave your comfort zone almost permanently

KAY GIRE

**66** If you are serious about setting up your life coaching business, I would recommend that you look at the course as having two parts: one part – developing your skills as a coach and the other part – developing your business skills. Do the two parts simultaneously so that by the time you receive your certificate, you can easily slip into the role of 'SUCCESSFUL ACCREDITED LIFE COACH'.

As far as support to set up your business goes, the marketing course and the teleclasses give you loads of ideas as to how you can make the public aware of your presence. But this aside, setting up your business is ultimately and entirely in your 'extremely capable' (even if you don't believe it) hands.

You will decide and set-up the type of company you want, you have to design and write the material for your website, and create a business plan. This part of the journey is not easy – sometimes filled with frustrations – and it may become extremely uncomfortable as you have to leave and work outside your comfort zone almost permanently.

But when the rewards start rushing toward you, you will feel the satisfaction that only your endurance could give you. You will then know that you are *there* and it's all down to you! **99**

To achieve your goal, your life may sound like a perfume counter – full of Passion and Obsession, leading to Joy.

**JOHN-ROGER AND PETER MCWILLIAMS**

# 10  Coaching in the workplace

> Most employees are motivated, energetic, committed, enthusiastic and loyal – except for the eight hours they work for you.     TOM PETERS

'COACHING IN THE WORKPLACE' is a term which covers a wide range of activities from very high level leadership coaching programmes involving senior managers and executives to – at the other end of the spectrum – a coaching 'approach' or culture which focuses on achieving results through encouraging people at all levels to find their own answers and take responsibility for their actions. This is in direct contrast to the traditional 'command and control' style of management that was common until recent years.

As coaching in the UK workplace is still relatively new, only a limited amount of research has so far been undertaken into how it is being applied, the role it plays, and the benefits which result. However, what studies there are show that coaching is growing in popularity among businesses as a tool in the promotion of learning and development. What's more it is believed that unlike some other forms of training, coaching has tangible business benefits.

A research survey conducted by the Chartered Institute of Personnel and Development (CIPD) in 2004 found that: *'Coaching is seen as a more effective method of learning than training courses'*, *'96% of respondents thought that coaching is an effective way to promote learning in organisations'*, *'coaching is also seen as a key way to reduce "leakage" from training courses and therefore improve their effectiveness'*.

In addition, The Coaching Study 2004 – a research project conducted by The University of Central England into coaching in over 100 blue chip UK companies – reported that *'Although current practice is variable there is clear evidence that a more systematic and structured approach to the use of coaching will contribute greater value.'*

Coaching, then, is effective and is seen to be working, even though there is still some way to go in respect of the framework in which it operates and the generation of measurable results. Regardless of how it is applied, however, coaching has at its heart a concern for people and their well-being and fulfillment. It appears that finally, business owners and leaders are starting to realize that happy, well-motivated employees are more productive, and that appropriate work/life balance is an essential requirement for all staff at all levels:

## When fatigue turns to burnout

JACQUI KNOWLES

66 I started my working life as an accountant and then progressed into management consultancy. I had worked my way up to quite a senior role and was working abroad most of the time, project-managing large financial systems implementations.

About four years ago I started suffering from excessive fatigue. Eventually I resigned from my job, thinking it was the constant travel that was causing the problem. Through research I realised that I was suffering from excessive stress/exhaustion and decided to find out more.

I signed up to study for a Diploma in Stress Management. Wow, what an eye opener! It soon became apparent to me that I was going through something called burnout, which is quite a debilitating condition. Although I was quite ill I was relieved to finally understand what was wrong.

On completing my diploma I was asked by the training company if I would join them as an associate trainer. I hadn't thought of using my new qualification to earn my living, but then thought 'why not?' I was studying for my coaching accreditation at the same time and thought it would be good if I could combine the two.

At first I made the mistake of turning my back on nearly 20 years of business experience; I thought a clean break would be best. But I soon realised that the experience was what made me 'me' and I would be a fool not to use it. As the stress management/awareness training took off, I saw that I could use my coaching expertise with those trainees who needed additional support after the training, or indeed to offer one-to-one stress coaching where training wasn't appropriate.

As a result I have just designed a well-being programme (a much better word than stress I think) that incorporates training and coaching on a one-to-one basis for work-related stress. I am currently piloting the programme with a company in Manchester. I also offer Executive Coaching (using a great deal of my business expertise) and my first client was one of my practice clients! I am now targeting senior managers who have to travel a lot as part of their job; again I am using my experience as well as my qualifications to help others, and clients seem to like this, it's a great USP. **99**

In the workplace, coaching is concerned with enabling individuals to retain control of their lives, thereby increasing their motivation and most importantly, reducing the amount of negative stress which working life produces. If every employee realises their innate potential and drive, then the collective results are dramatic, as Stephen R. Covey (author of the 'Seven Habits…' books) indicates:

*'An empowered organisation is one in which individuals have the knowledge, skill, desire, and opportunity to personally succeed in a way that leads to collective organisational success.'*

## The disappearing trainer (or the case of the shrinking ego)

ALAN MATTHEWS

**66** I've spent the last 13 years involved in training and it's fascinating to see how things have changed over that time. It's also interesting to consider how I have had to try to change myself in recent years to keep up; in particular dealing with the blow to my ego of realizing I'm no longer the focus of attention.

Here's a brief history of training:

*Stage 1:*

Trainer as expert imparting knowledge.

Main skills – presentation, explanation.

Ego boost 10/10.

*Stage 2*

Trainer as facilitator: creating a learning environment.

Main skills – designing activities, handling group discussions.

Ego boost 6/10.

*Stage 3*

Trainer as coach.

Main skills – questioning and listening.

Ego boost 2/10.

The emphasis has shifted over the years and the central role of the trainer has receded. Now it's not about me and what I know, it's more about them and their needs. If I'm honest, part of the satisfaction I used to get from training was being seen as an authority and being praised for my presentation and communication skills. Now I've had to learn new skills and the irony is, the more skilled I get at coaching the less it looks like I'm doing.

However, the main satisfaction I get from training is seeing people discover things that can have an impact on their lives or their work. I want to make a difference, to bring out the best in people. And I know I'm actually being much more effective now if I use coaching techniques.

The training is more relevant, it's based on the learner's needs, and it brings about more long-lasting change. Now, instead of suggesting what they should do or think, I ask questions, get them to think for themselves and gain their commitment to real change instead of filling in compulsory action plans at the end of generalised training courses. When the learning comes from them it lasts and it changes their lives and that's why I do this job in the first place. **99**

Coaching for the executive or manager in the workplace can create a total win/win situation for all parties involved – staff, manager and employing company. Coaching allows the manager to let go of the perceived need for them to 'have all the answers' and be responsible for everything. By entering into partnership with employees through coaching, the manager enables them to seek new and creative solutions, reach their own – group and individual – decisions, set their own individual and team objectives, take ownership of delivering what they have decided, and approach their work with fresh enthusiasm.

> Imagine life as a game in which you are juggling some five balls in the air. You name them – work, family, health, friends and spirit and you're keeping all of these in the air. You will soon understand that work is a rubber ball. If you drop it, it will bounce back. But the other four balls – family, health, friends and spirit are made of glass. If you drop one of these, they will be irrevocably scuffed, marked, nicked, damaged or even shattered. They will never be the same. You must understand that and strive for balance in your life.
>
> BRIAN DYSON, CEO, COCA COLA ENTERPRISES

Whatever is actually done, the fact of simply demonstrating the qualities of a coach – being supportive, open, and non-judgmental – can bring about a sea change in the culture of the workplace.

Such an approach creates mutual trust, understanding and high levels of responsibility and integrity. Because of their increased level of involvement in the decisions surrounding their jobs, employees feel a greater degree of loyalty to their employing company, their colleagues and also to the management that allows them to operate in this way. The process is positive, and as a result, employees are not constantly looking for reasons to criticise, blame or act uncooperatively. Rather they will tend to view management with respect rather than resentment, and demonstrate support rather than sabotage.

A further benefit for managers using coaching is that staff learn more quickly and retain that knowledge more if they discover through experience rather than by being told or shown. As part of this process employees may find new and more productive ways of doing things rather than simply following tried and tested (and often tired and outmoded) procedures. Coaching can also enable teams and individuals to set their own priorities and reorganise work processes, which can result in time savings and quality improvements.

## My journey towards coaching in the workplace

JOHN BLAKEY

❝ My journey has exposed me to the way that managers are taught and the ways that managers lead in practise. I have been deep into the annals of the education system through studying for degrees in science, management and IT and through training as a counsellor and life coach. I have immersed myself in a business career that took me from the public sector into the private sector. From a large utility into one of the fastest growing, small companies in the UK via a global manufacturer. From supervising unionised, blue-collar workers in Coventry to leading multinational IT project teams comprising some of the most capable people of my generation.

Through all of this, I have learnt one spellbinding lesson – there is a better way to develop people than that which pervades the majority of our institutions today. That 'way' is through coaching. I believe coaching represents the future cornerstone of management and leadership in a world where people are giving up on traditional methods and searching for something new. It is a phenomenon that the business world has an opportunity to proactively embrace but risks ignoring at its peril.

I cannot state this challenge better than Sir John Whitmore in his book 'Coaching for Performance': *'Many people believe that a major shift in the attitude and role of business is inevitable. Will this come about by a series of managed course corrections as businesses learn to accept their responsibility, their true meaning and purpose or will they continue their blinkered pursuit of wealth at any price until they run into barricades manned by ordinary people with higher demands and aspirations?'*

Or somewhat more bluntly put by Jim McNish Head of Executive Development at retail group, Kingfisher (quoted in the Financial Times) *'Human beings want to love their organisations – they don't want to work for a set of b******s'!*

I dedicate these words to those bright eyed people who refuse to let the fear culture win, who are modelling coaching behaviour and values and who are working around the world to breathe the life and soul back into business – don't give up!

### Don't give up!

At 22, my first management appointment was a baptism of fire. I was asked to manage twelve militant service engineers in the Coventry depot of British Gas. This was at a time when the unions were strong and it was not common for a 22 year old to be managing people twice his age! This was the University of Life in all its glory and I used to quake each morning as I braced myself for the ritual confrontation, 'game playing' and ups and downs of each day.

The learning curve was vertical for many weeks but gradually the team accepted me and we built a degree of trust. The performance of the team started to improve and notorious slackers started to emerge from their shells to make a contribution. In my naïvety and idealism, I was determined to manage these people as I myself would like to be managed. But, not for the last time, I also felt the pressure to be 'tough', to 'sort people out', to shout and to rant. And as performance improved, I encountered resistance from my own management who saw it all as a foolhardy experiment and a dangerous precedent.

Nine years later I was working for an organisation that had been voted Britain's most admired company two years running. I really thought I was going to join the bluest of the 'blue chips' and was ready to be hugely impressed. I had expected to see all the leading edge management theories being implemented and lived out on a daily basis. I expected that it would show up my previous employer, British Gas, as a 'stodgy', ex-public sector company that was just playing at business. Unfortunately, I was disappointed! I knew that I could not live long in that environment and that, as a project manager in the IT department, I was not in a position to change it. After eighteen months, I left.

## A fascinating experiment in leadership and management

And then came 121 Consulting! This was a 70-person business when I joined it in 1996. It was led by a young and charismatic entrepreneur called Iain Barker who was later to become one of the wealthiest people in the country. At that time, Iain was just a normal guy who wanted to make a difference. From my very first encounter with 121 Consulting I knew I had stumbled upon a fascinating experiment in leadership and management. The German co-founder was wearing an earring, blonde ponytail and polka dot shoes when he interviewed me. On the wall was a picture of Jimi Hendrix. Wow!

121 Consulting had found itself caught up in the huge growth in the IT market in the nineties. The people who led it were not traditional managers. They did not have MBA's, had not undergone corporate training, they were not versed in the so-called 'real world' of business. But they were armed with huge energy, self-belief, knowledge and a sense of fun.

As I adapted to this company, there were times when I thought it was anarchy, that there was no respect for the management, and that it was amateurish. I judged and judged this company from my MBA/corporate perspective and then one day, I realised what was really going on – there was NO FEAR in this company!

I realised that it had been fear that had driven the organisations that I had worked for in the past. Sometimes, this fear was explicit, sometimes it was hidden, but it was always there, pervading and defining the culture. There was no fear in 121 Consulting and although it was chaotic and amateurish and 'disrespectful', people were blossoming and achieving great things. They were growing and leaping out of their comfort zones knowing that they were protected by this fearless culture.

It was here in 1996 that I first came across coaching. I was dispatched to a course on Advanced Change Management, which involved me sitting in a hotel room in the New Forest with a coach for five whole days. By the end of the second day I was all set to leave and dismiss the course as a waste of time. I could not get my head round what it was all about and every part of my rational, 'left brain' was screaming 'get away'. But I stayed – and on the third day something in my head 'just 'cracked open' and everything I had ever believed or learnt was suddenly irrelevant and misguided.

It was like the whole scaffolding collapsing in one go. It felt like I was losing my mind and, of course, I was. But in losing my mind I found something that was much more important and it was this that then propelled me forward in every aspect of my life. It was like being swept along on a huge waterfall of energy that had been released from the dammed up recesses of my consciousness. This was my personal experience of coaching and from this point on, I committed myself to understanding this phenomenon, developing the skills to practise it and sharing this with as many people as I could find. But I had a lot to unlearn first!

In the workplace, 121 Consulting became one of the fastest growing private companies in the UK in the late nineties. Its staff grew from 70 to 440. I found myself working in Scandinavia for two years and leading a number of audacious, multinational project implementations across Europe. I became a Director of the company in 1998, achieving a lifetime ambition.

In 1999, we sold the company to a global IT service company. At a personal level, it was both a dream and a nightmare. On the one hand, I was suddenly financially independent, on the other, I lost the culture that I had cherished and valued. The experiment was over and we were swallowed up by another corporate machine.

### Working hard to develop a more balanced lifestyle

For two years I ploughed on, despite my reservations. It was at this time that I started to plot my escape from the corporate world to find a 'better way' of developing people through coaching. I developed my first 'grand plan', which was that I would leave after three years and use this time to work through book after book on the subject of psychology, spirituality and self development. I immersed myself in learning t'ai ch'i. I gave up my ambition to develop a career in the company and kept my head down lest I was sucked into it all. It helped keep me sane as I started to 'dig my tunnel'.

But then, in July 2001, I was asked if I was interested in a more senior role in the company – the only role I had ever harboured any desire to do! It involved becoming a Managing Director of a global systems business focusing upon developing international business. It was a fantastic opportunity, but it caused me much internal anguish as to whether to accept the role or not.

Outside my job I was working hard to develop a more balanced lifestyle and to get out of the 'rat race'. This new role would involve considerable international travel and I knew how time consuming and tiring this would be. I was also wary of the corporate culture of the company and that I might be expected to conform. Finally, I wanted to study for a counselling qualification and develop my coaching plans for the future. It was a dilemma.

It became clear that I had to work out what I wanted and ask for it. I had to be prepared to set my own limits and stand by them if necessary. I had to take responsibility for my life! Scary stuff.

So when I met with my (possible) future boss, I listened and listened and listened. Then I took a deep breath and spoke from the heart. I made him aware that I did not share the current values of the organisation, that I was not ambitious to be a future main Board member, that I had other interests in my life which were important and that I would love to do the job but I would only do it if I could work a four day working week.

When I finished speaking I expected the sky to darken and lightening to strike me down. Instead I heard my future boss say 'I don't see that as a major problem. I trust you to put in the hours you need to get the results.' Blimey! This was nothing short of a miracle.

This arrangement allowed me to continue to travel in my job and be 100% committed to it for four days a week. On the fifth day, I worked on other areas of my wheel of life. Sometimes I took the children to school and picked them up, sometimes I met my sister for lunch, sometimes I went racing with friends and always I worked on my counselling and coaching learning. One day, I even found myself watching a film on TV at noon – shocking!

### Developing a new perspective on my work

There were times early on when I felt pangs of guilt at this arrangement and my demons stood at the door taunting me – 'You should be working harder', 'You should be worried about your job', 'You should be concerned that others will do better than you'. At its worst, I could feel myself breaking out in a cold sweat. But I stuck with it and gradually my new life became normal to me.

I found that my energy levels and motivation increased. I found a new perspective on my work that put it into context and reduced the stress. Rather than detracting from my performance at work, this new sense of well-being started to help me be more effective over a sustained period of time. I had to prioritise and focus and manage my time carefully but things still got done.

In the early days of my new role, as I built a network of new relationships, I was accused of being 'too nice' and not driving people hard enough. This reminded me of all the corporate lectures I had received in the past. There was a huge temptation to lurch towards using fear to get things done. A huge feeling that if I did not do this I would not be accepted and I would fail. Failure was something I did not want but neither did I want to resort to using fear to get results. I still believed in a better way.

### I wanted to prove that coaching delivered results

Outside of work I had completed my counselling qualification and had started a coaching course with Rivas Palmer. The course helped build my confidence to keep progressing with a coaching style in the workplace and I started to coach people privately on all aspects of personal development and growth. This helped keep my energy levels high for my corporate work. Gradually I started to see the impact on others around me in the workplace.

Whilst much of my coaching at work was informal, I initiated a regular formal program of coaching for the immediate members of my team. These sessions followed the TGROW model and I applied the full theory and practice of coaching, as I knew it. I enjoyed the sessions and got positive feedback from the team. Moreover, the sessions focused on specific work achievements and goals and could be directly related to 'bottom line' benefits. I wanted to be able to prove that a coaching approach delivered 'hard' results and the team opened their minds to this possibility.

At the end of two years in the role, I was able to present some outstanding results to the Board of the company: I had succeeded in growing my business by 38% in an overall market that was shrinking! We had won our biggest contract ever (£31m) and had expanded the business out of Europe and into USA and Asia. I had increased the investment in my direct team five-fold and been rewarded generously.

The same people that had called me 'too nice' now thanked me for tremendous results and asked me how I had done it. Of course, I gave coaching all the credit.

Now I had made my point I felt it was time to revisit my 'grand plan', resign and become a full time coach. Well, that was the plan....

I built up all my energy to give up a corporate career of 20 years and all the investment that I had made in that. I carefully calculated how much I would need to earn to keep myself and family in bread and water, I took a deep breath and... I resigned.

Then strange things happened.

I found myself being asked by the CEO if I would stay on for 12 months to 'kick off' a strategic coaching programme in the company. Something I never would have predicted! This was a total shock and had, once again, upset the 'grand plan'. But how could I turn down the opportunity to coach at Managing Director / CEO level in a global systems company? How could I turn down the opportunity to be the first Director of Coaching in a UK plc?

So, once again, I have ripped up the plan and today I am several months into developing several strategic coaching initiatives for the company focusing on succession planning, new appointments, business turnarounds and culture change. It is a privilege to nudge the culture towards a coaching mindset, towards a 'fearless' environment. There is a long way to go and many risks along the path but I am finally giving my all to something I believe in and have worked all my life to achieve.

There will be no more 'grand plans' since I have learnt that it does not work that way. On the contrary, 'it' works through a much simpler mechanism – an open commitment to a better way, finding your unique role in that process and having the courage to jump into the unknown on a regular basis.

### Business can be a vehicle for creativity and good

When I think of a future vision for the workplace I refer, once again, to the words of Sir John Whitmore in 'Coaching for Performance' – *'My optimism is rooted in the positive yearning of indomitable human spirit. I believe that business is somewhat off track, though not yet off the rails. It feeds off and appeals to our lower nature, power and greed, but at the same time it can be a vehicle for our creativity, aspiration and the will to good. Business is the most powerful man-made organising force on earth and along with education it is the vehicle through which transformation can most effectively come about, driven by the human spirit. But business urgently needs to get back on track and align itself with higher and more caring human values.'*

In large public businesses managers are separate from employees and owners are separate from managers. It is tempting for each to treat the other as objects rather than respect each other as human beings. In these environments it is all too easy for 'strong management' to replace 'principled leadership' and for fear and greed to become the pervading motivation within the organisation. This reveals an underlying belief that people perform best when they are frightened and when rewards are scarce. Everything in my being and in my experience rejects this belief as limiting and hopeless.

So where does coaching fit in? Coaching empowers people to take action and liberates them from limiting beliefs. It raises awareness of personal values and fears and expects people to take responsibility for their thoughts, feelings and actions. It is based on a belief in the unlimited potential of each person. Consequently, 'coached' individuals will not be motivated by fear and believe that everyone can be a winner.

Initially, people may operate in isolation at different levels of the organisation. They will create 'bubbles' of principle-centred leadership, pockets of creativity, inspiration and superior results. Sometimes these bubbles will reach the leadership roles of the organisation and so grow bigger and envelop more people. Sometimes they will be burst by the aggressive reaction of threatened power bases. But as the coaching phenomenon grows and taps into the latent potential of more and more individuals, the bubbles will gradually join up and take hold and become a collective truth.

At some stage, the 'tipping point' will be reached and whole organisations will reinvent themselves in the coaching spirit. This change will not come about from the top down; it will be a truly bottom up phenomenon. As such, it will be sustainable and painless because it will not depend on creating new losers or on fighting for power.

We each have a choice regarding the role we want to play in this 'velvet revolution'. The choice will arrive when we decide whether to spend our hard-earned corporate dollars on another IT system or a global advertising campaign or to invest this money in coaching. Only then will we have accepted our responsibility for creating the workplace we want and accepted that no one else will act if we ourselves do not take the first, decisive steps.

Finally, it is left to each individual to work out when 'banging your head against the same brick wall' becomes more painful than taking that first step towards real personal change and liberation. I know from my own experience that this cannot be forced upon anyone or preached or lectured. Similarly, I do not believe that armies of coaches can invade organisations and overthrow the old ways. But when people do reach this point in their own self-development, the coaching profession can be on hand to facilitate, respond and nurture. I look forward to helping in this process. **99**

As this book is being written, Rivas Palmer is taking the next logical step for the development of its own business and launching a Corporate Coaching Division to both focus on training in-house coaches and to develop programmes through which quality coaching can be introduced into the workplace at all levels and in all types of business.

Increasingly in the future, businesses will experience external pressure to modify and improve working practices. This will come both from legislation and changes in social and cultural conditions and attitudes. For example, at the end of 2004 new regulations covering stress in the workplace will be added to the existing mountain of legislative requirements that employers must implement.

> Concern for man and his fate must always form the chief interest of all technical endeavours. Never forget this in the midst of your diagrams and equations. **ALBERT EINSTEIN**

But any employer who may be considering introducing coaching in the workplace as a 'quick fix' panacea to use as a defence against disgruntled, litigious employees is missing the point.

The real benefit of coaching is that when properly introduced, implemented and monitored in the workplace by qualified, experienced coaches it does away with the blame culture that currently pervades our society. Anyone who truly embraces a coaching ethos knows that whatever happens, 'blame' is an inappropriate response.

## Coaching should be mainstream, not just part of the HR function

**ANN SKIDMORE**

❝ I was aware of coaching right from childhood because of the way I used to be with my friends. Although I didn't have a name for it then, I now know that's what coaching is all about. That's how I found out about it in terms of my own life; but I really got into it professionally about 12 years ago because my background is human resources.

I run a lot of training courses and have done all my career and every time I did a course people would come up to me in the break and say 'I really enjoyed the course,' and 'You inspired me' and 'I've got this issue in my life' – and I'd be coaching them in the breaks! I had taken a degree in psychology and as part of the degree I had a mentor, which was very useful, but I realized a mentor does slightly different things, in a different way to a coach.

I knew that coaching would be more valuable in terms of my profession because it's about the client being in control whereas with a mentor it's more 'Look at what I've done – and you can do it too.' So these days, I mentor people but I do it from a coaching perspective. When I'm mentoring I call myself a coach/mentor. One of my clients at the moment is a Director on a main board and he hired me because he wants to do what I'm doing – running his own company, but equally he wants coaching to be able to do it for himself.

Being a coach/mentor to senior executives in business is something I now do more and more. Also, when I go into companies now, I'm often hired to run a particular event like a leadership or performance management programme and alongside that I do coaching beforehand to find out why people are coming on the programme and what they want from it, and coaching at the end to find out what they gained from it.

More often than not the companies aren't keen on that in the beginning because they think the coaching element is just going to cost more money. However when they've seen the success that results from training combined with coaching, they really see and appreciate the value.

What coaching does in the workplace that nothing else can, is push the responsibility and the accountability where it needs to be. Often when I start coaching, what I hear is, 'Oh, it would be fine if it weren't for my manager', or 'It would be fine if it weren't for my team'. But through coaching, people take on more responsibility and accountability, and acknowledge the fact that if their boss or their team is a problem, it's up to them to do something about it, even if it's just to raise the point that they're unhappy.

To me, that is the fundamental difference between coaching and anything else in development and training. It makes people much more accountable, much more responsible.

### Self-esteem and confidence are universal issues

Coaching really is about 'not ducking the issue'. I admit I'm a challenging person; I'm very empathetic and my clients tell me I'm very humorous, but I won't let them off the hook. If they've got a crisis, I think I'm very understanding of that and pace them through it; but in the longer term they hire me because they want results, not because they want someone to say 'There, there, isn't it awful?'

The way a client presents their issue in the beginning and what the real issue turns out to be, are often quite different. I explain to clients that this might be the case, and that it's absolutely okay. I say, look, whatever you hire me for initially is absolutely appropriate and you might want to get some quick wins on that, but then there may be a fundamental issue which is holding you back that you will want me to help you with too.

The main issues for my corporate clients are usually those around business life, about managing their time, managing their projects and managing people. But fundamentally, whether it's in life coaching or corporate coaching, the main issue that people want coaching on – although they don't always know it – is their self-esteem and confidence. No matter where they are, no matter how successful, this issue always seems to be there in the background.

Usually only about 20%–30% of people know that they're lacking in confidence at the outset, we don't tend to talk about it in the UK. I think it would be of great benefit if we did. I believe one of the most courageous things you can say is, 'My confidence is dipping at the moment and I just need a bit of a boost.'

In the last five years I've coached nearly 6,000 people and there is no one person I have ever met who in my opinion has got it made. They temporarily think they have then life deals them a couple of shocks. Richard Branson would say the same, Sir John Harvey Jones would say the same, Bill Gates would say the same – you can be incredibly successful but if you take your eye off the ball, you're arrogant. You've got to really keep your eye on that ball and keep it moving.

The majority of people that I coach at the top of organisations are male. That's sad for two reasons. First, I think it's sad that men often don't feel there is anybody else in their organisation that they can approach for help. Second, having been a senior manager myself, it's sad that there aren't enough women at the top because I think they've got a lot to contribute.

In business or in life, women are very receptive to coaching and are more likely to consider hiring a coach. Men are a little slower to come to coaching, but when they do, God bless them, they open the floodgates. They tell me everything. One compliment I had last week from just such a client was, 'You know, you're just like my best friend, you're an honorary bloke'!

### Coaches need to get better at measuring success

In years to come I would like coaching to become really mainstream and not be seen just as part of an HR function. I'd like organizations to view it as having their corporate coaches, either external coaches or their own, as a real business need. I'd like to see coaching become much more acceptable with people holding coaching forums and coaching meetings and sharing best practice. I'd also like to see better analysis of how it was helping the business, benefiting the bottom line. That's ultimately how it will become mainstream in the workplace.

I'd also love to see more coaching in schools, because I think those are workplaces for children – and I would like to think there would be a point in the future where you don't need people to be coached because they have grown up knowing that it's an absolutely appropriate function. Sports people have their own coaches and look how well they do. And wouldn't it be great if people grew up accepting themselves, having bags of confidence?

I think what will get in the way are those traditional views that coaching is a cost rather than an investment, and not analysing the true benefits over time. There are still many negative views on spending any money on training and development, and that is why our profession has got to get better at measuring success.

I do it by setting benchmarks. For example, I'll work with a company looking at what their staff turnover is and their staff absence rates and their morale index before we do anything. It's not scientific, it's not brilliant, but at least it allows me to say, 'Well these are the measures before we intervened with coaching and training, and here are the measures afterwards.'

### It's not just a route for getting rich quick

Some people today who are delivering coaching view it as a route to getting rich quick and I think that's a very dangerous attitude for the profession, for clients and for those people themselves. I'm keen not to dissuade anybody, but they need to be sure that their own ethics are in the right place – that they want to get into corporate coaching because they have something that they can contribute and they want to make a difference in the corporate world.

Motivation is crucial because the corporate world is very quick to sniff out people who are in it just for the money; I've seen some coaches crash and burn that way. But if someone has the right reasons for doing it, I would want to help them get into the corporate world. Some people think that they can't if they haven't got a corporate background, but that's not always relevant.

I would say to anyone, 'Use what you already have, use your unique talents, skills and attributes and market yourself accordingly.' There's room for all sorts of coaches in the corporate world if you have the right motivation. 99

# 11 A funny thing happened...

> At the height of laughter the Universe is thrown into a kaleidoscope of new possibilities.    JEAN HOUSTON

A FUNNY thing happens when people train to be coaches… they change! Not only do they change, which is interesting in itself, but along the way, some strange, amazing and amusing things happen to them – as this chapter will demonstrate.

## 'Hurricane Mike' breaks London's West End

MIKE MOSS

66 Whether you're a fan or have never watched a snooker game before, 'Hurricane' is an absolutely gripping, emotive piece of theatre – telling the life story of one of Britain's most charismatic sporting heroes, Alex 'Hurricane' Higgins.

As snooker loopy myself and an admirer of Alex, I had to get tickets for the performance. At the door, we were asked if we wanted to buy some of the raffle tickets on offer. What was the incentive? Four people, whose tickets would be picked from a hat, would get the chance to play the great man himself at the end of the show. As you can imagine, I jumped at the chance to buy two tickets and pulled out from the hat, yes, wait for it, number thirteen. No way! And to top it all, it was a Friday!

At the end of the show, the pool table came onto stage and the great man, Alex 'Hurricane' Higgins stepped forward. Immersed in the atmosphere, I felt a prod in the ribs from my girlfriend, 'it's you, they've called number thirteen' she said.

My nerves got the better of me and I shakily went up; this was my first time ever on a West End stage and I was about to perform in front of hundreds of people. Suddenly, lights! camera! action! – my turn to play Alex had arrived.

The commentator cheekily introduced me as 'Mike the Magnificent' and Alex shook my hand and asked me what I did for a living. With all the gusto that I could muster, I answered, 'I'm a life coach.' He asked me what that was and for once, I fluently managed to explain what I did, to which he wittily replied, 'I could do with one of those to help me stop gambling and womanising.'

Throughout the match we exchanged lots of jokes and banter. It was an entertaining game that had the audience on the edge of their seats. I am pleased to say I was the only one of the four individuals picked, who beat him that night.

For those of you who know the game of pool, you will understand when I say that the run of balls favoured me all the way – even though the black ball was a safety shot that went in. Alex thought it was a trick shot – my lips are sealed.

One thing I will say, is never fear the number thirteen. It worked for me. Not only was it a Friday, not only did number thirteen get picked but I managed to successfully speak to people about life coaching at the end of the show and hand out thirteen business cards that night... how much luckier could I get? 99

One of my initial fears about coaching was that it might turn out to be evangelical and scarily, intense (incense, chanting... that sort of thing) or equally as bad, worthy but dull. Fortunately, it's neither of those things. Coaches are just normal people – albeit some of the funniest, most cheerful people I've ever come across; it does one's heart good just to be around them.

## Using humour to break through fear and anxiety

BELINDA MOLLROSS

66 I've done a lot of personal development workshops, a lot of them around spirituality, raising awareness and, taking control of things. And what I've found with almost every therapy that I've used, is that it's purely a tool for the individual to get to where they need to get to, or to find what's within them.

The ritual – the massage, the drops, the tablets, whatever – is actually unimportant; what's important is the client's mental attitude and how they feel and change while being involved in that ritual.

Humour, to me, is one of the most important things in any relationship. As the comedian Victor Borge said, 'Laughter is the shortest distance between two people.' It's a way of breaking the state your clients are in. If the client can look at what they're doing with a bit more humour, it changes the level of fear or anxiety that is going on around whatever the issue may be so they can then see through it, and to a degree, detach themselves.

My whole approach is fairly humorous, for example there is a popular saying, 'A lot of water has gone under the bridge since then' – my preferred wording of this is 'A lot of bridges have gone under water since then' – it seems to fit the situation better!

Humour really does bring dramatic results. I frequently get calls that end up with the person saying, 'I always feel so much better after I've spoken to you.' Most of the time with my clients and students, we laugh: Don't get me wrong we have very effective coaching sessions, but if you see the funny side of things, you relax and at the same time see the opportunities that might be there.

Sometimes though, things just spring to mind that amuse me but I have to bite my tongue not to say anything. For example an old school friend of mine rang and said she'd found God, and my immediate thought was, 'I didn't know he was lost!'

### Coach training is not an academic process

As well as coaching private clients, I also mentor student coaches, which I really enjoy. They're my little fledglings, my little chicks. It's fascinating to see how each student grows through the process, and it doesn't matter what their background has been. They can be extremely well qualified and virtually a coach already through what they've previously done, but going through the process, doing the course, moves them to a completely different place.

The one thing I would say about coaching is that it's not an academic process. If you treat it as such you're going to miss the whole point; to train to be a coach is experiential … you learn and you grow through the process.

I don't think I've met a student yet who hasn't dropped their bundle somewhere during the course, but then we pick things up and we keep going. Usually it comes from a very deep-seated realisation that they have to look at everything again, through different eyes. It's quite a major stage when that happens – they're putting down their old way of thinking and then when they get that sorted, they pick up the new one and move on.

Those who go through that are generally the ones who make the best coaches because they really have taken it on board and experienced the whole process for themselves

Basically, I see my role as being a catalyst. I have the by-line 'take control of your life' which is where I think most people have a problem; they perceive that there is no choice, control and no way out of the situation they're in. But working it through, you realise that it's always in your control. You might not necessarily like what the choices are, but there are always choices.

My deepest belief is that you have two choices; one is to do it the easy way, the other is to do it the hard way. Those are the only choices. Quite often, because of our upbringing, we have been told that if you're going to get anything you've got to work hard for it. So we tend, from unconscious habit, to take the harder way because that means the end results will be that much more worthwhile. Well, it would be just as worthwhile if you took the easy way and got it! I'm all for that.

Quite often the hard way involves worrying about things that actually haven't happened. It's that old saying about worry being interest paid on a debt that hasn't been incurred. Most times it's completely pointless. Things move so quickly; you plan on a worst-case scenario and tie up all your energies – and then it doesn't come to fruition. Great, you feel good, but you've wasted all that time and energy worrying! It's just not worth it.

I would never say 'Don't plan', or 'Don't look at all aspects of things', because that is too naïve – but don't dwell on them, either. Deal with them where possible, be aware of what pitfalls may arise, but dwelling on them is giving them energy – and it's sapping yours. Give the energy to the good possibilities.

The main thing, I believe, is to have fun! My message to everyone is

'Don't be so serious'. When you take everything so dreadfully seriously you restrict possibilities. Believe me, I can even make businessmen laugh! They can see the funny side of what they do. I was talking to one the other day about how he'd prefer monkeys as his staff; we had an hilarious discussion about what the downside of that might be!

## You can't be responsible for other people's reactions

So, sometimes there is merit in pursuing something that is ridiculous just to lighten things. And sometimes you have to realise that actually there isn't anything that you can do about a situation except change your attitude towards it. You've been hitting your head against a brick wall trying to change something or someone and nothing is happening. But if you just change your attitude, suddenly it doesn't seem to be so painful anymore. It may just be your perception, or sometimes something seems to have spread out from your change of attitude so that they actually do change.

What it boils down to is that you can't be responsible for other people's reactions, only your own. If you say and do things with the best of intentions, then people have got to live with how they choose to react. Other people can put their own wishes onto you and sometimes, as a result, they don't want you to change. They fear change and if you suddenly start to get your life in order and things are working for you, that really scares your friends and family because it means 'If you can do it, that means its possible for me and that means I've got to leave all these nice familiar problems behind and sort things out – and that's scary.' So what they start doing is pointing out what's wrong with you now that you've changed –'You've gone all weird!'

The thing with coaching is that provided a participant is willing, they can be coached. But for some, change is just so scary that they are not willing to participate. They hate what they've got, they say they want to change it – but to actually do something about it is more than they can bear. These people, even in a coaching session, are carried along by the idea of change, but actually doing something about it is a different thing altogether.

Coach or client, I believe it's all to do with enjoying the journey. It's the same with goals, its not really achieving the goals; it's the journey to the goals that's important. It goes back to the easy way and the hard way, it doesn't have to be hard and if it's hard, sit back and think, 'Is this really where I should be going and what I should be doing, or is there an easier way of doing it? **99**

Obviously there is a lot of laughter and humour associated with coaching for the simple reason that it is a process that encourages people to push themselves outside their comfort zone. In such situations, you can get frustrated, feel inadequate and embarrassed, but anyone with a sense of the ridiculous will also tend to laugh at themselves – after the event, if not at the time!

> Laughter and tears are both responses to frustration and exhaustion. I myself prefer to laugh as there is less cleaning up to do afterwards. **KURT VONNEGUT**

As someone once said, the reason humans were the only creatures given the ability to laugh is that there is so much about the human condition to laugh about. There's also the truism about the fact that in many situations, if you didn't laugh you'd cry. Someone else said, 'Blessed are those who can laugh at themselves – for they'll have endless amusement' – how right they all are!

So, what an honour and delight it can be for a coach to be able to laugh with a client who is recounting their escapades and adventures as they experimented with something new. How rewarding, as time goes by and they progress, to find the client's nervous laughter replaced by laughter created by the joy of living and a heightened awareness of the goodness in the world around them.

## Down at the swimming baths...

**LAWRENCE NELSON**

**66** What follows is true (honest guv), is not exaggerated and only struck me as being funny once I had thought about it, rather like an Alan Bennett story.

I feel that the story has a moral in that whilst many more people are now aware of life coaching, there are still many who are not!!

My wife was telling someone that I was a life coach when, quick as a flash came the reply 'Oh yes I know, down at the swimming baths, does he enjoy it?'

I would stress here and now that I emphatically do not sit coaching someone over the phone resplendent in swimming trunks, cap and goggles. **99**

# Ultimately we control our own success

LINDA ORCHARD

66 Suffice to say I was in the middle of perhaps the worst year of my life. With circumstances pulling the rug out from under my feet, my confidence and self-esteem were at an all time low. I had lain down and relinquished all control over everything. My career, for which I had studied hard and had loved, had been altered immeasurably so that it seemed my qualifications, experience and skills had been devalued and were no longer respected or deemed useful.

The over-riding message I was hearing, both in my work life and personal life was 'put up or ship out'. The recent actions of my partner and my subsequent reactions to them, had left me with no self-respect or trust and I was really struggling.

Months before, we had discussed getting a dog. Much as I love dogs and did indeed want to have one, I knew that at that time I could not cope with providing for its needs, plus two young children, a husband and a job. However, I had been worn down and agreed to the idea and was secretly really keen. When things started to go wrong at home though, there was an unspoken agreement that it just wasn't going to happen anymore.

Though very disappointed, with the future so much in the balance and the possibility that I would now have to cope on my own with the children, the house and a job which was now making me very unhappy, I accepted it and set about convincing myself that we should absolutely NOT get a dog.

Then, at the end of August, either out of guilt or to convince me that things would be okay, my partner presented me with a puppy on my birthday. We named him Archie and ultimately it was Archie, the West Highland Terrier puppy who became responsible for me discovering Rivas Palmer.

It was a real comfort for Archie to be around when I was left on my own night after night. The consequence of this though, was that the majority of house training came down to me. One morning, on the newspaper-covered kitchen floor, right by the back door, upside down, and in between a wet patch and a pile of unmentionably smelly stuff, I saw an advert in the paper on the floor that caught my eye.

I don't even remember exactly what it said, I just saw it and knew I had to stop and take notice. I had been drawn towards an advert (thankfully still clean and dry) for a Rivas Palmer open day that I extricated from the mess and kept in my pocket for the rest of the day. Of course I couldn't go because:

- it would be scary and unknown,

- it might actually be taking control of something,

- the open days were in London and Manchester and I was in Northamptonshire which obviously made it quite impossible for me to get there (note the excuse for not moving forward), and

- what if I *were* to go and it looked like it *could* be possible for me to get involved? Even more scary! Talk about miles outside the comfort zone!

Anyway, I kept the advert and Archie, having played his part in my fate, learned to control himself and stopped presenting me with worrying opportunities of a possible new future.

Things became worse at home and I kept digging out the advert again from time to time to take another look. I came to the conclusion that my comfortable life with the nice husband, children, car, and house might no longer be reality. One day I thought it wouldn't do too much harm to look on Rivas Palmer's website to see if any more open days were being held. That would be safe enough because, of course I knew I wouldn't do anything about it.

Uh oh! What now? Was this fate, destiny, or a kick up the backside? I found that not only were they holding another open day, but:

- this time it is only about eight miles from my house,

- it is on a day and time that I will be able to go without having to worry about a babysitter,

- it is in a manageable two weeks time, and

- unbelievably it's free!

OK, where are the excuses I need now? I managed to come up with the following (isn't it amazing what you can say to yourself when you're desperate?):

- Well, if it's free, it can't be any good (memo to self – remember this thought when charging clients!)

– With my previous training I could easily set myself up as a coach (unqualified) without having to pay for another course. (This was also pointed out to me by a colleague at work who has a similar problem with stepping out of the comfort zone!)

– It could turn out to be like a time-share presentation.

Somehow, though, bearing in mind that something in my life *had* to change and that I was only going along just to see, I decided that I would check it out but would stay armed with my utter determination that they would really have to convince me this was something special if practical, cynical Linda was going to get drawn in. 'I'm not daft, no one's going to take me for a ride,' I thought to myself. Loosely translated this of course means 'No-one's going to get me to do something new or scary with *any* element of risk whatsoever involved'!

So along I went and found one of the most welcoming (without that irritating over-the-top-stuff) bunch of people I've ever met. These people exuded a kind of calm belief that yes, life isn't always as you would want it but it *can* be okay if you take responsibility for your own life, accept what's happening and see that you do not have to be reliant on others' thoughts, behaviour and actions for your happiness.

It was the demonstration of a coaching session that really did it for me, though. Just to see what *can* happen when you ask the right questions and how 20 minutes worth of help towards real insight can alter a problem that's been holding you back for years. I could do this. No, not only that, somehow I would find the course fees and I *would* do this.

The following day, I got up to get the children ready for school and realised that I could hardly stand up. My husband had taken the week off work to find somewhere else to live so he got them to school that day and the rest of the week, while I shivered and sweated and slept my way through the flu, feeling both very ill and devastated by the fact that he was leaving.

A few days later just about when I was beginning to think straight again, my course books arrived and I read a book that consolidated everything I had seen at the open day. It convinced me that coaching really was the answer to many things. It was time to stop banging my head against a brick wall and playing the victim. I needed to take responsibility for what was happening, see the chances presented to me as opportunities rather than problems, and trust that it *would* be okay.

So, what if we hadn't had problems in our relationship? What if Archie had not arrived and hadn't needed house training? What if I hadn't been ill that week? What if these awkward things had never happened? I'll tell you. I would still be stuck in a rut, still bemoaning the fact that someone had changed my job without my say so, still kidding myself that I had to make do with whatever was invading my comfort zone.

As it is, I am well into my coaching journey. It's hard work, it's scary and it requires a willingness and motivation to change that I never knew I had. I have learned a way to cope with imposed change and have turned into a more positive, open and dare I say, spiritual person. I have met some wonderful, amazing people who all have their own baggage but have found the guts to embark on this exciting adventure. I'll tell you something though. If you could buy this trip at the travel agents, someone, somewhere, would be making a FORTUNE! 99

> I once had a full conversation with someone about coaches. He seemed bemused by what I had to say; I eventually realized I was talking about coaches but he thought I was talking about buses. I quickly excused myself from his company before it ended in a nasty pile up.
>
> ANON.

## Who said coaching was a serious business?

You can whistle them while you work, and hum them when you're happy (or not) ….
Here, courtesy of Kirk Halinson, is the ultimate coaching chart …

**Life Coaching Rock**

| Track | Artist |
|---|---|
| 1 Don't Give Up | Peter Gabriel (featuring Kate Bush) |
| 2 Better Days | Bruce Springsteen |
| 3 I Still Haven't Found What I'm Looking For | U2 |
| 4 I Believe in You | Neil Young |
| 5 Absolute Reality | The Alarm |
| 6 Changes | David Bowie |
| 7 Story Of A Life | Harry Chapin |
| 8 What Are You Going To Do With Your Life | Echo and The Bunnymen |
| 9 Have A Little Faith In Me | John Hiatt |
| 10 Keep On Growin' | Derek & The Dominos |
| 11 I Just Don't Know What To Do With Myself | White Stripes |
| 12 You Can't Get What You Want (Till You Know What You Want) | Joe Jackson |

# 12 'Look mum, I'm a coach!'

> If we did all the things we are capable of doing, we would literally astound ourselves.
>
> **THOMAS EDISON**

FOR MOST people embarking on coach training, the big question that they really want answered is: 'What's life like after coach training; what will change when I'm a proper, accredited coach?'

The answer, of course, depends on your expectations. There are those who have been astounded by the difference coaching has brought to their lives; those who have made small but significant changes; those who have altered internally while still continuing along the same external life path; and those who have had an amazing impact on others.

One of the common messages that comes out of all the stories of those who have completed their coach training is that it is very much just the start of the process. Although some may have embarked upon their journey with the idea that it had a beginning, a middle and an end, what they have all come to realise is that the 'end' rapidly becomes displaced by a universe of unlimited possibilities.

## The best decision I ever made

**GERALDINE THALMESSINGER**

66 I gave up my job at Andersen Consulting to retire on a yacht in the Mediterranean. However, life never goes as planned and that relationship broke down leaving me back in London with no job, a house to run and two grown-up kids. After three months at home during which I lost a lot of confidence, I heard from a friend who'd also left Andersens that she'd become a life coach and I was tempted to go along to an open day.

Although I knew nothing about coaching, I'd never read any books or known anyone who had been coached, I nevertheless decided that this was for me. On the course I was extremely nervous and self-conscious and concentrated on making sure that I wrote absolutely everything down which meant that I didn't take it in. Fortunately however there were two extremely good and supportive HR people also on the course and with their help I got through the first practical session, even though I was petrified that I just couldn't do it.

Since then I've never looked back. I've developed a property business and now own 13 properties, including one in Spain, which I certainly wouldn't have done without coaching. Other positive outcomes are meeting Natasha at a coaching event that ultimately led to me becoming a Rivas Palmer founder member.

It was certainly the best decision I've ever made and every day I still think 'Who knows where else it will lead?' It's taken me a long time to find my niche, but now that I have, it's all I've ever wanted. **99**

## Adding value to people's lives and growing myself

**DEVI PATEL** | **66** Without coaching my life would have been totally different. I would probably be working for the same company I was four years ago, still not knowing what I wanted to do and hating my job. I didn't really know what I was passionate about – so coaching has really made a difference in my life. I can honestly say that it is the best thing I have ever experienced.

I can see very clearly why I have chosen being a coach as a career:

– Because coaching has made a difference in my life.

– I am totally passionate about people living their dreams.

– Coaching unleashes the power of an individual.

– Blind spots are recognised.

– Coaching allows individuals to go beyond what they think is possible

Now I really feel happy, energetic, alive and excited 90% of the time – and this is a result of coaching, so this leads me to aspire to create that feeling in other people. Also, because I know from my own experience that coaching actually works, I am able to carry out a coaching career with commitment, passion and integrity.

In my opinion, being an extraordinary coach needs a total passion for coaching, a love for people, the commitment to make a difference, and an ongoing drive to transform areas of your own life that are not working as well as you would like – hence coaches must have a coach.

As a coach I feel that I am adding value to people's lives and at the same time growing myself – I am constantly being coached in areas of my life that I would like to transform. 〞

Once accredited, students go on to practise coaching in a wide range of niche areas, either as a part-time or full-time business. The common thread that runs through their stories is that the coaching itself and the benefits it can bring to others far outweighs the importance of financial return, even though some coaches establish very profitable businesses right from the start.

## If I had all the money in the world I would still coach

SHARON CRAWFORD

〞 The day I was given a particular business card was the day my life changed for the better! A friend gave me a card for Natasha Palmer at Rivas Palmer and said, 'I think you'd make a great coach, Sharon. Why not look into this?' So I did.

Since my excellent training, where I made contact with some wonderful people, I have specialised in coaching single professionals, to help them build a better relationship with themselves in order to have better relationships with others. It is immensely rewarding and satisfying.

However, the personal and spiritual development I have experienced will far outweigh any financial benefits I will ever receive from this chosen path. If I had all the money in the world I would still coach; I feel like I'm finally giving something back to others, as well as to myself. In fact I feel that everyone around me benefits indirectly because they're getting a much truer reflection of the real me. 〞

Of course, even coaches aren't immune to the many obstacles that life and the Universe can present, but there is ample evidence that those who have had their passion and determination re-awakened through coaching, have found the strength and resilience to overcome whatever hurdles lie in their path.

# Stepping-stones or stumbling blocks?

**LYNNE SCURLOCK**

66 *'Challenges can be stepping stones or stumbling blocks. It's just a matter of how you view them' (Anon)*

This is a powerful quote for everyone, especially a coach. Life would be boring without any challenges but how we view those challenges is how we measure our achievements. Stumbling blocks or stepping-stones, do we jump them, move around them, allow ourselves to be sidetracked or give up all together?

Now I am accredited, starting out as a coach feels like stepping out on a great journey. Where I end up may be entirely different from my initial goal, but I will keep reviewing what is important to me. At present I aim to have my own holistic centre in five years, where I can offer life and wealth coaching, as well as letting out rooms for other like-minded individuals to offer services such as Reiki, Reflexology, Meditation, Yoga, etc.

Within a short time of completing my final assessment, a major challenge (illness) was to stop me in my tracks for weeks. It proved an ideal opportunity for my study buddy to coach me on what really mattered to me. I could have given up on my goal, but I took the opportunity to re-evaluate my values and what I truly want.

I am now jumping from stone to stone, getting my life back together again, both personally and professionally. I have taken the time to put together how I want my business to look – letterheads, welcome packs, a website and a bi-monthly newsletter. I have even managed to link up with other students to form a small local support group.

I am concentrating hard on getting myself known and my practice clients have been referring new people to me. Friends have offered fantastic support and wherever they can, have put up my leaflets in their places of work or have passed on my name.

A year ago I was just starting on my studies, now I am preparing to run my own business, I feel like I am flying high. Taking those initial steps to get there is a slow process; challenges do get in the way. Stepping-stones or stumbling blocks, it is a matter of how you view them. I truly believe if you do a small bit at a time, you will get there. 99

## To me coaching means removing barriers

DENISE HEATH

❝ Coaching is reshaping me into the positive, independent, focused, determined, fun-loving person I used to be. It is also moving me further forward to the successful entrepreneur/businesswoman I know I can be. Coaching has also worked to enhance my spirituality, helping me to look deep inside to achieve what is my life's purpose.

I'm using coaching to set up my own coaching practice, 'Working with people striving for balance and fulfillment in their lives'. I'm also noticing how many times I ask 'coaching' questions in conversations, especially with one of my biggest energy drainers – my sister!

To me, coaching means 'the removal of barriers in achieving all that I strive to achieve, in all areas of my life'. It is a process which will enable me to work with like-minded, positive, determined, warm and passionate people who are open to ways that they can be empowered to make those internal shifts and positive changes in their lives the way that they want.

Coach training has enabled me to regain my self-respect, determination, direction and passion for life. I've benefited from regaining my self-confidence, the ability to shine and belief in myself. Also, the ability to define, take action on and achieve my goals. I've found a new network of friends and colleagues, too. ❞

## Coaching has changed me

TIM WATTS

Coaching has changed me as a person. I now have a more balanced life and enjoy more and better quality time with the family. I am communicating better than I have ever done before, feel a deeper love for others, and am better organised and use my time more usefully,

My memory too, is enhanced now I am so much more aware of things that are happening or being discussed. My wife used to say 'You can't remember because you didn't listen in the first place,' and I have to admit, she was right! I also think that partly that is because men generally have very poor memory for detail.

I have to say I am very mellow now and much more self-confident. I can stand up in front of hundreds of people and engage them; in fact I feel I have a frightening level of confidence. Although previously I was a very successful person, I now feel oodles better about myself.

My drive and determination is now notable. I used to wait for something to be presented to me before I grabbed it. In fact sometimes I used to be accused of under-achievement and I can see that was probably right. Certainly I was stressed, but these days I feel totally in control and right here and now. **99**

> People are always blaming their circumstances for what they are. I don't believe in circumstances. The people who get on in this world are the people who get up and look for the circumstances they want and, if they can't find them, make them.
>
> **GEORGE BERNARD SHAW**

If you have read through the rest of this book, you should now be under no illusions about what coaching can and cannot do. It is a tool, not a magic wand. It is a process that enables people to find their own answers, not one that causes them to rely on other people deciding what is best for them. Because of this, those who have been coached are set free. They know they have the power and the ability to do, be and have whatever they want. It will inevitably take time, perseverance and hard work, but they know their vision CAN be achieved.

## The ability to build a better future

SUE CLARK

**66** Do you often find yourself thinking things like, 'one day I would love to…','I wish I had the courage to do…','my life could be so much better than this…'? Well, I know I am biased, but I want to take this opportunity to tell you how coaching has changed my life for the better!

Before I became a coach I decided to *BE* coached to see how it worked and *IF* it worked – after all, if I was going to be one then I had to know what it was like! I knew it was going to come at a price but I had got to a stage in my life, in my early 40's, where I was sick and tired of 'making do', of not fulfilling any ambitions because I was scared. I wanted to make something of my life but I just didn't know what to do or how to do it. It was mostly lack of self-belief that held me back.

So, I booked four sessions with a coach and within one month I was a changed person!

The process enabled me to think for myself, make things happen and finally take control in areas of my life that I had for so long wanted to 'shake up'! As a result I undertook coach training, still a bit scared, but I did it and proved to myself that I can do anything I put my mind to. Life coaching isn't a magic cure and doesn't provide you with advice or answers but it does give you the ability to build a better future.

I launched my own business and have enjoyed helping other people, and this year I took the plunge and started studying with the Open University and am now in my first year towards a degree! I would never have done this had I not been coached and been helped to learn to believe in myself!

I am so proud to be a mature student and am soaking up new knowledge like a thirsty sponge. I still have some unfulfilled dreams and ambitions but now I am more trusting of my own abilities, I have also learnt to 'go with the flow' more, am less bad tempered and actually *like* who I am now (I used to be very grumpy most of the time and I was often depressed and lacking in motivation).

I know that opportunities will present themselves to me as life goes on, and I have such strong intuition now that I know what is 'right' for me. My experience with coaching has also rubbed off on my family. I have indirectly coached my husband without him knowing. He has been pursuing a more worthwhile career and is now working on a TV series at Pinewood Studios and we are all relocating soon to Buckinghamshire! My 15-year-old daughter has seen the changes in me and she too is taking more control of her future – she is writing her first novel and wishes to become a famous author!

So whatever you do, make a pact with yourself today – find just one goal or dream that you would love to fulfill, set a date to realise your dream and work out what you need to do to reach that goal. You *can* do it. Tell yourself you can, and you will! **99**

## Coaching complements my spiritual work

ANTONIA BEHAN

**66** The skills I learnt with Rivas Palmer enhanced my natural coaching abilities and taught me excellent models for working with clients. Rivas Palmer offered more than I imagined; their marketing workshop run by Gary Lafferty filled me with so many ideas and plans I was buzzing for weeks. Gary Lafferty is a true inspiration, he is so full of life in his workshops, 'bouncing off the walls' is the term,

I think! This workshop gave me a solid foundation for launching a successful business.

I completed the course in about four months and since then I have found life coaching complements my spiritual work beautifully. I am now confident about what I do, knowing that my work truly empowers others to change their lives and achieve their dreams. I believe every coach is in love with their work and feels the joy, the love and the beauty that touches the hearts of their clients, as each client is given permission to be true to their self, to honour their heart and follow their dreams.

I feel life coaching is a truly spiritual practice delivered in a down-to-earth and practical manner, accessible to anyone ready to make a positive change to their life. 99

## The journey of a lifetime

MARIE STEVENS

66 Training to be a coach requires dedication, a belief in yourself and the desire to make a difference. Having been told by a client that I had changed her life, that she was the happiest she'd been in years and that she couldn't thank me enough, was one of the most moving and humbling experiences I have ever had.

Coaching for me is the journey of a lifetime, a voyage of discovery and a wonderful way of being; I hope it will never end. 99

## A more dynamic and expressive life

JANNA CRAZE

66 For many years I worked in the Film and TV industry as a set-painter, taking three years out when I was thirty to study for a degree in English Literature. Making the final break from the film world, once I was accredited as a life coach, was a leap of faith – but one that has brought me the fulfillment and challenge that I had been looking for.

I have had the privilege to be involved with Rivas Palmer since its conception and am very proud to be one of the Founder Members. One of the reasons that life coaching was attractive to me as a career was a core belief in people's ability to change. Coaching complements all other areas of my work beautifully as I contribute to realising the full potential of others. **”**

## Clarity, fulfilment and satisfaction

PAUL STONEHOUSE

**“** I have been a manager in Financial Services for most of the last 12 years, and most recently a partner in a firm of Independent Financial Advisers. Although I enjoyed what I was doing, there was a gap for me in terms of real fulfilment and satisfaction. I decided that I wanted to consolidate and refine my previous coaching experience, and learn a structure for building a successful coaching practice.

Having trained with Rivas Palmer I am now in the process of putting into place many of the structures I learned on the course and have never felt more relaxed, at peace with myself and fulfilled, knowing that being a professional life coach is exactly right for me at this point in my own life journey. Completing the training programme has given me a very strong foundation for creating my new career as 'the Clarity Coach', and helped me find and become established in the life I am made for. **”**

Many references have been made throughout this book to the three aspects of the human persona – the intellectual, spiritual and physical. Although we have dwelt in detail on the intellectual and spiritual sides of coaching earlier in this book, the physical element should certainly not be overlooked as these next stories indicate:

## Goal setting at the gym

TONYA WILLIAMS

**“** I run my own Personal Training business, *Innergym* in North London, travelling to people's homes. Having been in the fitness industry all my life, I know the benefits and shortcomings of my profession. One of the most common complaints amongst personal trainers is that whilst we have lots of technical knowledge, actually achieving the client's goal to the full isn't that easy.

It was during coach training that I realized the reason clients didn't accomplish their goals was because we all lacked this one key element – EFFECTIVE COACHING.

Since qualifying as a life coach I have doubled my client base (as well as my income). Rather than simply meeting the client and embarking on a fitness program, I now take the time to establish with them a really SMART goal, clear, precise and realistic. Thanks to the training, my rapport with clients is excellent, so much so that very few have left me – despite having achieved their goals already.

The training has also enabled me to create something unique. I actually coach the client while I am exercising them.

Once we've established our GOAL, we can then discuss at the beginning of each session the REALITY of their situation. I can then use the exercises (for example a two-mile run) to explore the OPTIONS. ('Okay Jean, at the end of this minute, can you think of one option you could try to take you a step closer to your goal?') And so on, until we've completed the two miles – that's 20 options, by the way!

Finally, my client can finish the workout by choosing which of the OPTIONS they WILL do…and we can end with a few stretches that enable them to visualise being, doing or having their goal.

I am really excited about my company's future. Through my technical and coaching skills I have elevated my business and myself to a considerably higher level of expertise than is the norm and have recently increased the size of my ambitions accordingly. I feel that Rivas Palmer has played – and continues to play – a significant part in this. **99**

## Knock out idea

RICHARD PRICE

**66** Even before I became accredited I had the idea of combining my two passions – coaching and sport – and working towards specializing in coaching in the sports arena using the principals of psycho cybernetics.

Currently I'm working on a strategy for coaching boxers, and in connection with this have been in communication with the ex-world champion Barry McGuigan who seems interested. I'm really hopeful that this will lead to great things. **99**

# Marathon Man

GEOFF BAYLEY

❝ On my coaching residential weekend back last September, there was a moment when we were all challenged, on the spot, to commit to doing something that would be life changing in the next seven days. The fact of having to declare it to the other 30 or so budding coaches added gravitas. Wishful thinking had to be owned up to and transformed into action. There were witnesses with memories.

Overcoming my initial 'rabbit in the headlights' state, the idea of running the London Marathon popped to the front of my mind and continued to resist my rational brain's attempts to dislodge it. Before I knew it I could hear a voice, my own, sounding sincere and enthusiastic as I shared this commitment with the gathering.

Let me make it clear, I am not a runner. Admittedly I had occasionally been known to jog, in the vain attempt to lose some weight when the summer holidays were approaching, I had also had bouts of commuting the 12 miles to and from work on my bicycle, but most of the time I was as slobbish as the next couch potato.

My rational brain however had craftily inserted a get-out clause: 'I will apply to run the London Marathon in the next week.' That only meant I had to *apply* – it didn't mean I actually had to do it… Perhaps it was my imagination but I could sense a degree of weariness, a scepticism in the faces of some of the tutors; they had heard empty promises before…

I knew that most people who apply don't get accepted the first time and this gave me a degree of comfort, indeed confidence.

I was now working from home; my commute required a walk down the landing to the bedroom/office. On energetic days I might make it to the garden gate as I took the trash out. My body was shutting down for winter hibernation and thought of the marathon was now no more than an Indian summer aberration.

Mid-January, I got the news I had been offered a place. A fragile elation was overwhelmed by anxiety about the size of the task and the time available. Better not tell anybody; I could still turn it down. Yet if I was going to do it I had to start fund-raising for Shelter, my chosen charity, pretty quickly…

Lots of water passed under the bridge, but guess what? I did it! I've got the medal, I finished inside five hours, and it was a truly great day. I'm hooked; all I want to do now is to run more marathons.

Hey, this life-changing stuff works if you let it. **99**

One of the truly overwhelming messages that has emerged whilst compiling this book is how grateful everyone is for having been introduced to coaching and supported in their journey by Rivas Palmer. The book is no idle puffery. Those who have contributed to the book are but a sample of those who have been fulsome in their praise and gratitude. Many more positive tales would be here if not for space restraints and the practical difficulties of pinning busy people down to extract their stories.

> To laugh often and much; to win the respect of intelligent people and the affection of children; to earn the appreciation of honest critics and endure the betrayal of false friends; to appreciate beauty; to find the best in others; to leave the world a bit better; whether by a healthy child, a garden patch or a redeemed social condition; to know even one life has breathed easier because you have lived. This is to have succeeded. **EMERSON**

I am sure there must be one or two people out there who aren't entirely satisfied for whatever reason, but I know they won't have been allowed to go away from Rivas Palmer without every effort having been made to put things right.

As someone who has spent a lot of time working in and around the arena of quality and service standards (and an ex-Rivas Palmer customer myself), I am highly impressed by the whole package. It is heartening to think of how many people are now going out into the marketplace setting up their own coaching businesses, or going back to the workplace, with this level of quality, ethics and commitment as their standard.

Personally, my wish is that Rivas Palmer continues to flourish so that this happens even more.

## Coaching was what I had been looking for

JANET PALMER

**66** When a friend gave me a 'self-help' book to read after my marriage had broken down, I was unaware these books existed. This book opened up a whole new awareness in me – I was enthralled and couldn't put it down. I quickly became addicted, reading every book I could find!

These books helped me understand myself better and gave me the courage to undertake counselling. With this came great personal growth – quite literally transforming my relationships, my life and myself! I became fascinated by self-esteem and personal development issues and have spent more than seven years reading, learning and studying. I began to feel I wanted to work in an area of personal development, but did not want to do counselling.

Then a friend booked me onto a Rivas Palmer open day. I had never heard of life coaching and had no idea of the purpose of the day. However, as I listened and learned I knew this was what I had been looking for. I booked onto the next residential weekend, and came home filled with excitement and lots of work to do. I set myself a goal of 9–12 months to achieve my accreditation, but in fact found the work so compelling and interesting, that got there within five months!

I am now building my business, enjoying every moment and finding the world of Life Coaching the most positive and rewarding experience – I simply love seeing my clients grow! **99**

## Realising what I was put on this earth to do

WENDY GLASSOCK

**66** It has taken me until now, age 42, to realise what I was put on this earth to do. My personal journey started three years ago when I became a Reiki healer.

I never felt I had the confidence to 'be' anything. I was good at motivating people, genuine, sincere, caring. I was a qualified reflexologist – I had done counselling, nutrition and voluntary work; all of which was to do with making people feel better, but still somehow felt it wasn't 'it'.

About a year ago I became depressed. At this time I had a leaflet through the door about a NLP course that talked about self-limiting beliefs and becoming the person you want to be. I was interested, but it required a big commitment in terms of time and money. Nevertheless I signed on the course, but on the first day felt I had made a big mistake as everyone else seemed very important, very sophisticated and representative of a different world to mine. There were lots of big words and technical terms, but I battled through.

The next day we did the Time Line exercise (linking the past to the future and asking how you are going to get there) and it blew my socks off, it was fantastic. I set myself a goal to be a lifestyle consultant by November 2004.

However, underneath it all I was still depressed and troubled. The course finished in January 2004 and at that time I had a breakdown. However, a couple of months later I saw an advertisement for Rivas Palmer in the newspaper and my husband said 'This is what you were meant to do'. Since then, the change in me has been phenomenal.

I went on the April 2004 residential course and since then the feedback from my clients has been exceptional and uplifting. It has made me feel more open and a lot less worried about being vulnerable. As a friend of mine once said, 'With you, it's not the fear of failing that holds you back, it's the fear of succeeding.'

I now realise that this is what I was born to do. Coaching is more gentle than NLP and is to do with helping people to realise their full potential in any situation. Counselling is listening; coaching is making people take action.

If I was advising someone else about whether or not to take up coaching, I'd tell them to get all the basics in place first, start at the beginning and go through and do each stage of the training properly. I've been really impressed with Rivas Palmer and through them have made many new friends.

A bonus is that I've lost one and a half stones in weight since I started, simply because I'm no longer eating for comfort. I've also had to step outside my comfort zone in many ways, for instance, I've had to conquer my fear of driving on motorways in order to get to coaching meetings.

Coaching opens you up to many things that you can do. Perhaps one of the biggest differences I noticed about the coaching world is that it is not about materialism – who's got what' and 'who does what' – it's about being yourself and reaching your true and full potential. 99

# The journey has been a great privilege

TIM PRIDEAUX

❝ I came to coaching rather later in life than some trainees, but even so, I still found it an incredible process for finding things out about myself that I didn't previously know.

I succumbed to the lure of coaching late in 2002 when a friend of mine sent me an advertisement for a Rivas Palmer open day with the comment 'This sounds just like what you want to do.' As a result, I rang them on Christmas Eve, and was not only very impressed to find someone committed enough to be answering the phone on that day, but was immediately bowled over by Natasha's enthusiasm and passion for coaching.

I signed up for the February 2003 course and completed it last October, having been slowed up somewhat by a knee operation along the way. I've also completed the Corporate Coaching Day and as I now have a paying client, I feel that my coaching career is really underway.

Prior to embarking upon my new mission, I'd had a long career with WH Smith as Head of Personnel in their Distribution Division. Latterly, I was in control of the company's community affairs and was seconded from this to a role with Business in the Community. After this, I became a Director of a career outplacement consultancy, and I have also been a Magistrate for 20 years and a non-executive Director of the Surrey Police Authority (helping monitor quality standards).

I now fervently believe that coaching is a very cost-effective way of developing people. In years to come my dream is to be busy helping people through coaching and to have found a way to introduce coaching to those organisations which, by their very nature, are unable to afford normal coaching rates, for example the charitable and voluntary sectors

Finally, for anyone – particularly anyone more senior – who may be considering whether to embark upon coach training, I have to say that I'd wholeheartedly recommend it. Certainly the learning process is good for you, and in addition, I have experienced great benefits in terms of de-cluttering my life, and personal organisation.

> I've also been highly reassured to discover that we're all human and no one is perfect – whether coaches or clients. Along the way I've also met some wonderful people and consider that the whole journey has been a great privilege. Yes, at times it's been a struggle – but ultimately it's been very good for me. **99**

So there it is – 12 chapters of stories about how coaching has changed lives – all for the better. Whatever your reason for reading this book, I trust that you have found this uplifting, even if you take away nothing more.

If you are a coach, I hope the book has given you renewed enthusiasm and zeal for the good you can do. If you are considering becoming a coach, I hope this has encouraged you. If you have been coached, I hope your experience was positive and worthwhile. And if you have yet to experience coaching and are struggling with some issue in your life, stress, or general unease, I hope you may now feel inclined to give coaching a try. You may find that it may be the start of a very special journey for you too…

Finally, my favourite quote, attributed to Andy Warhol, and one which seems a fitting conclusion:

> They always say time changes things… but actually you have to change them yourself.
>
> **ANDY WARHOL**

# Coach contributors

**Lateef Badat**
**ALB Coaching**
Motivational coaching –
guaranteed results
Tel: 07813 808429
Email: info@albcoaching.com

**Geoff Bayley**
**GB Qualitative Research**
One-to-one change of career
coaching for professionals
Tel: 07739 466744
Email: geoff@bayleyresearch.com

**Antonia Behan**
Inspiring you to heal yourself
and live your dreams.
Email: antoniabehan@aol.com
www.psychicdiary.com

**John Blakey**
**121coaching**
Specialists in international and strategic
corporate coaching programmes
Tel: 01564 829135
Email: johnblakey@121coaching.com

**Yamie Boakes**
Email: yamie@bluenowhere.co.uk
67 Wood End Avenue, Harrow,
Middlesex. HA2 8NU.

**Graham Boocock**
**Unique Advantage Coaching**
Business, executive and personal
coaching for achievement,
effectiveness and change.
Tel: 0845 644 2424
Email: Graham@UniqueAdvantage.co.uk

**Lesley Buckeridge**
2 Riverside House, Burcot, Oxfordshire
OX14 3BY
Email: Lesley.Buckeridge@hotmail.com

**Sue Clark**
**BTR Coaching**
Email coaching service for all personal
issues. Support for Coaches.
Email: sue@btrcoaching.com

**Ginny Colwell**
**Coach and Healthcare Consultant**
Particularly interested in Healthcare
and Senior Management coaching
Tel: 077404 36463
Email: ginnycolwell@blueyonder.co.uk

**Sharon Crawford**
**Motivus International**
Singles coaching & start up/
small business executives in IT.
Tel: 07799 772076
Email: scrawford@motivusinternational.com

**Katie Day**
**Creating a Brighter Future**
Women working in a man's world,
raising their self belief
Tel: 0845 458 3105
Email: solutions@kday34.freeserve.co.uk
www.creatingabrighterfuture.co.uk

**Sharon Dennis**
Career coaching for nurses and
health and fitness
Tel: 07961 354381
Email: sharondennis550@hotmail.com

**Steve Elshaw**
**Resource One**
Professional networking, corporate
and personal development.
PO Box 3681, Dronfield,
NE Derbyshire S18 2WS
Tel: 01246 412111
Email: steven@resource-one.co.uk
www.resource-one.co.uk

**Claire Elston**
**Claire Elston & Associates**
Corporate and Business Coaching,
achieving greater work/life balance
Tel: 01702 611076.
Email: claire.elston@virgin.net

**Robin Evans**
**Robin J Evans and Associates –**
**Corporate and Executive Coaching**
Working with companies and individuals
who genuinely want to embrace change
Tel: 01782 661169
Email: rje@robinjevansandassociates.com
www.robinjevansandassociates.com

**Emma Fairchild**
Tel: 0114 2580958
Email: ecfairchild@aol.com

**Susie Fletcher**
Life Coaching, coaching after counselling,
personal development
Tel: 01789 414704
Email: jefsufletcher@btinternet.com:

**Kay Gire**
**Nirvana Life**
Empowering unfulfilled professionals
to define, create & live blissful lives!
P O Box 373, Blackburn, Lancs, BB2 5ZE
Tel: 0845 226 1974
Email: kay@nirvana-life.com

**Wendy L Glassock**
**AIM HIGHER**
Personal and Rehabilitation
Tel: 07940 370867
wendyglassock@aol.com

**Alisoun L E Gort**
**Rise Coaching**
Life/work balance –
Post counselling coaching
Tel: 01386-840848
Email: alisoun.gort@virgin.net

**Kirk Halinson**
**Trust and Reward**
Career and Executive Coaching
Tel: 020 8573 3868
Email: kirkjohn@tiscali.co.uk

**Denise Heath**
**Positive Direction Coaching**
Working with people wanting balance
and fulfilment in their lives
Tel: 01895 813254
Email: positivedirection@tiscali.co.uk

**Jacqui Knowles**
**Jacqui Knowles Associates Ltd**
Corporate wellbeing and performance
coaching for senior managers and teams.
Tel: 0845 226 1516
Email:  jacquiknowles@onetel.com

**Gary Lafferty**
**Building Success**
Tel: 0845 564766
Email: info@buildingsuccess.org

**Sue Marchant**
Tel: 01895 233563
Email sue@sue-marchant.com

**Sian McDermott**
**Get Ahead Coaching**
Corporate and life coaching helping
clients to gain a competitive edge
2 Congreve Way, Stratford upon Avon,
Warks CV37 7JX
Tel: 01789 266708
Email: sianmcdermott@dsl.pipex.com

**Judy McGrigor**
**RAPPORT Coaching**
Motivational coaching for communication
excellence (personal & SME's)
Tel: 01452-857390
Email: judymcgrigor@btinternet.com
Chosen View, Churchdown Lane,
Hucclecote, Glos. GL3 2LR

**Julia Miles**
**Begin to Believe**
Personal and professional coaching
to take you from where you are to
where you want to be.
Tel: 07890 212006
Email: juliamiles@f2s.com
www.lifecoach-begintobelieve.com
www.beyonduni.com

**Belinda Mollross**
**Take Control of Your Life**
(you choose the area!)
– Personal, Business & Executive
Coaching. Mentor coach
Tel: 020 8761 0497
Email: coachwhisperer@hotmail.com

**Mike Moss**
Motivating mentor coach providing you
with inspiration to drive yourself.
Tel: 07903 392438
Email: mikey_moss@hotmail.com

**Lawrence Nelson**
**Eye 2 Eye Coaching**
5 Elm House barns, Carlisle,
Cumbria, CA4 OHS,
Tel: 016974 75448.

**Linda Orchard**
**Safety Net Coaching Services**
General coaching plus careers coaching
and relationship coaching
Tel: 01327 352014
Email: lifecoaching@safetynet4u.co.uk
www.safetynet4u.co.uk

**Jan Palmer**
**Coaching for Synergy**
Personal development, Education,
divorce, self-esteem, self belief, career
Tel: 0845 330 8242
Email: jan@coachingforsynergy.co.uk

**Natasha Palmer**
**Rivas Palmer**
Tel: 0870 0800 675
Email: Natasha@rivaspalmer.com
www.rivaspalmer.com

**Devi Patel**
Tel: 07956 69 3883
Email: devi@crystalclear-tc.com

**Maxine Peachey**
**Discovery Coaching**
Business and personal coach
Tel: 07900 608435
Email: Discovercoaching@aol.com

**Richard Price**
**Stepping Stones Life Coaching**
Improving performance in sport and life
Tel: 01252 33762
Email:
richard.price@acegolfer.freeserve.co.uk

**Tim Prideaux**
**Tim Prideaux Coaching**
Coaching in the workplace particularly
small and medium companies and charities
Tel: 01306 731326
Email: tprideaux@aol.com

**Sheree Rackham**
**Dynamism Coaching (Change,**
**Progress, Development)**
Helping you to lead the life you
know that you can.
Tel: 0797 0312026 (mobile)
Email: shereedynamismcoaching@fsmail.net

**Lesley Reader**
**Business and personal coaching.**
Tel: 07900 608349
Email: lesleyreader@hotmail.com

**Lynne Scurlock**
**Goalgetters Coaching and Training**
Wealth Coaching, Life Skills Coaching
and Training
31 Arlington Crescent, East Preston,
West Sussex BN16 1DS
Tel: 0845 4560965
Email: lynne@goalgetters.org.uk

**Mary Seabrook**
**Fresh Horizons**
Career change/development.
Life balance for professionals.
Overcoming anxieties.
www.freshhorizons.co.uk

**Ann Skidmore**
**Ann Skidmore Associates Ltd.**
Coaching and developing business leaders
for successful performance and results.
1 Poolfield Road, Lichfield,
Staffordshire, WS13 8EB
Tel: 01543-416242
Email: ann@annskidmore.com
www.annskidmore.com

**Christian Simpson**
**Evolve Life & Corporate Coaching Ltd**
Specialists in coaching within sales
disciplines of SME & corporates
14 Cheltenham Avenue, Upper Catshill,
Bromsgrove, Worcestershire B61 0RX
Tel: 01527 880 425
Email: chris@evolve-coaching.co.uk

**Marie Stevens**
Personal and small business coach
Tel: 01283 563664
Email: Mummypats@aol.com
The Burnt Gate, Hopley Road,
Anslow, Burton upon Trent DE13 9PY

**Pam Stokes**
**Rivas Palmer**
Tel: 01242 250036
Email: pam@rivaspalmer.com

**Paul Stonehouse**
**The Clarity Coach**
Working with people to be at their best
Tel: 02380 561079
paul@theclaritycoach.com
www.theclaritycoach.com

**Catherine Stratta**
**Coaching with Respect**
Corporate coaching:
productivity/performance improvement.
Life coaching: values, limiting beliefs.
Tel: 0845 490 0827
Email: c.stratta@coachingwithrespect.com

**Sarah Strong**
**Beyond Divorce**
Helping individuals to thrive – not just
survive-after divorce/separation
Tel: 0845 458 8184
Email: sarah.strong@tiscali.co.uk

**Helen Swanton**
Child Mentor (in central London)
Tel: 020 8877 2784
Email: helenswanton@yahoo.co.uk

**Geraldine Thalmessinger**
**Coaching for Life**
Tel: 0845 458 1086
Email:Gthalmessinger@aol.com

**Shaun Todd**
**The Caring Coach Company**
Unique products, gifts, support and
events to help coaches care
Email: shaun@thecaringcoachcompany.com
www.thecaringcoachcompany.com

**Meera Vohora**
**Yatra Life Coaching**
Expatriate Community, Business, Career,
Graduates and the Youth Community
Tel: 020 8944 9442
Email: mvohora@hotmail.com

**Linda Watson**
**'Wind Beneath Your Wings' Coaching**
Coaching novice managers and very old
hands (executives) for performance.
96 St Anns Road, Middlewich, Cheshire
CW10 9BZ,
Tel: 01606 833584,
Email: LWatson999@aol.com

**Tim Watts**
**Tim Watts Associates**
Corporate, Executive and
Personal Coaching
Tel: 01227 379920
Email: timwatts@timwattsassociates.com
122 New Dover Road, Canterbury,
Kent CT1 3EH

**Vanessa Westwell**
**The True Life Company**
Helping you to shine in your life,
work and relationships.
Email: vanessa@thetruelifecompany.com
11 Brook Street, Benson, Oxfordshire
OX10 6LQ

**Justine Wilkinson**
**Cardinal Coaching**
Unlocking potential to maximise
performance for Businesses and
Individuals
Tel: 01430 861617
Email:Justine@cardinalcoaching.com
www.cardinalcoaching.com

**Tonya Williams**
**Innergym**
Weight Management, Personal
Training & Postural Correction.
Tel: 07973 297840
Email: info@innergym.co.uk
www.innergym.co.uk

# Would you like to spread the word about coaching?

If you would like to use this book to help inform others about coaching or help promote your coaching business, we'd like to hear from you.

We'll send you a supply of promotional leaflets/order forms for the book which you then personalise by adding your name as an order reference. It's up to you what you do with them then – distribute them to friends, family or colleagues, hand them out at networking events, put them on notice boards or drop them through doors. Then, for every order form that comes back to us marked with your reference, we pay you 10% commission. You don't have to do anything except distribute the leaflets!
Tel: 0845 3306349   Email: enquiries@phosphorouspress.co.uk

## ℙℙ PHOSPHOROUS PRESS

If you have an idea for a book that you don't know what to do with, a half-completed manuscript that you don't know whether to develop, a fully-fledged typescript that you feel is ready to launch on the world, than you should contact us.

Phosphorous Press offers editorial and production services from initial typescript through to print with helpful and realistic guidance on marketing and distribution.
Tel: 0845 3306349   Email: enquiries@phosphorouspress.co.uk

---

**Rivas Palmer**
**Passionate about People**
Rivas Palmer offer a wide range of personal and corporate training courses and workshops. If you are looking for a coach we can put you in touch with trained and experienced coaches who can meet your needs. We also offer bespoke coaching and training programmes for companies and in-house training in coaching and mentoring for managers and leaders.

For further information visit our website www.rivaspalmer.com

Telephone: 0870 0800 675 or email: enquiries@rivaspalmer.com

---